Excellent resource that includes tools one can use when implementing a blended learning model. It clearly explains the role of a blended learning coach when it comes to professional development. Catlin Tucker emphasizes the opportunity to improve one's practice through coaching and a professional learning community.

—**Craig Yen**, *5th-Grade Teacher*

There is an urgent need to empower and support teachers through the implementation of digital tools and blended instructional models. In Power Up Blended Learning, *Catlin Tucker provides instructional leaders and coaches with the essential roadmap to develop internal structures of support within their schools. The time for teacher transformation is now, and this is the book to lead it!*

—**Tiffany Wycoff**, Co-Author of *Blended Learning in Action*, Co-Founder Learning Innovation Catalyst (LINC)

Technology can be transformative, but teachers need support to ensure technology is actually improving instruction. Catlin Tucker provides a clear vision for building a professional learning infrastructure to support teachers as they shift to blended learning and use technology thoughtfully and strategically. If school districts are not dedicated to helping teachers continue to learn and experiment, schools will remain out of step with the changes happening beyond the classroom.

—**Alice Keeler**, Math Teacher, Google Certified Innovator, and Microsoft Innovative Educator; Author of Multiple EdTech Books Including *50 Things You Can Do With Google Classroom*

Catlin Tucker has provided a critical "spark" in the blended learning conversation, shifting the focus from technology to culture transformation through ongoing teacher PD and support. As she has in her previous books, Catlin continues to offer practical strategies for high-fidelity implementation of blended practices, this time gifting instructional leaders with essential tools for guiding their professional learning communities.

—**Jason Green**, Co-Author of *Blended Learning in Action*, Co-Founder LINC

In Power Up Blended Learning: A Professional Learning Infrastructure to Support Sustainable Change, *author Catlin Tucker succinctly presents multiple options for blended learning professional development with a focus on coaching. Through the coaching lens, Tucker offers a clear explanation of the "what," a compelling rationale for the "why," and tangible guidelines for the "how" of professional learning for blended learning. This book is an extremely valuable resource for any person or organization looking to grow their individual or collective capacity and implement blended learning successfully.*

—Lisa **Westman**, Speaker, Consultant, and Author of *Student-Driven Differentiation: 8 Steps to Harmonize Learning in the Classroom*

Throughout this book, I found myself (as both a middle school teacher and as an instructional coach) saying, "Yes!" My copy is peppered already with stars in the margins and graphics circled for future reflection. Power Up Blended Learning *is not just for those who are coaching teachers. It's also for teachers looking for strategies in how to coach students. After all, giving engaging feedback that "sticks" is a responsibility that every educator has, and sharing engaging strategies and tools is a skill that is continuously evolving. This is an up-to-date and forward-thinking resource for both teachers and coaches.*

—Heather **Wolpert-Gawron**, 8th-Grade Teacher, Author of *Just Ask Us*

Power Up
Blended Learning

In loving memory of my grandfather, Ken Fermoyle.
You were the best editor a girl could have. I miss you every day.

For my children, Cheyenne and Maddox, who share their mommy
with teachers all over the world. You inspire me and my work.
I'm so proud to be your mom.

To my husband, Darian. Thank you for encouraging me to pursue my passions.
You make our life work and for that words are inadequate.

Power Up Blended Learning

A Professional Learning Infrastructure to Support Sustainable Change

Catlin R. Tucker

CORWIN
A SAGE Publishing Company

FOR INFORMATION:

Corwin

A SAGE Company

2455 Teller Road

Thousand Oaks, California 91320

(800) 233-9936

www.corwin.com

SAGE Publications Ltd.

1 Oliver's Yard

55 City Road

London EC1Y 1SP

United Kingdom

SAGE Publications India Pvt. Ltd.

B 1/I 1 Mohan Cooperative Industrial Area

Mathura Road, New Delhi 110 044

India

SAGE Publications Asia-Pacific Pte. Ltd.

3 Church Street

#10-04 Samsung Hub

Singapore 049483

Acquisitions Editor: Ariel Curry

Development Editor: Desirée A. Bartlett

Editorial Assistant: Jessica Vidal

Production Editor: Tori Mirsadjadi

Copy Editor: Shannon Kelly

Typesetter: C&M Digitals (P) Ltd.

Proofreader: Theresa Kay

Indexer: Scott Smiley

Cover Designer: Gail Buschman

Marketing Manager: Brian Grimm

Library of Congress Cataloging-in-Publication Data

Names: Tucker, Catlin R., author.

Title: Power up blended learning : a professional learning infrastructure to support sustainable change / Catlin R. Tucker.

Description: Thousand Oaks, California : Corwin, A SAGE Company, [2019] | Includes bibliographical references and index.

Identifiers: LCCN 2018018140 | ISBN 9781506396767 (pbk. : alk. paper)

Subjects: LCSH: Blended learning. | Teachers—In-service training. | Professional learning communities.

Classification: LCC LB1028.5 .T765 2018 | DDC 371.3—dc23 LC record available at https://lccn.loc.gov/2018018140

18 19 20 21 22 10 9 8 7 6 5 4 3 2 1

Contents

Preface

Technology is creating change in almost every industry. If the goal of education is to prepare young people to successfully enter the workforce, technology must be integrated into our schools to ensure students are fluent in it when they graduate. It's my belief that all classrooms will eventually blend online and offline learning. That blend will take many forms, but it *will* happen. Technology is radically changing how our society communicates, connects, and shares. This must impact the way we teach students if the skills learned in the classroom are going to be transferable to their lives beyond.

Ultimately, the impact of technology on learning depends on the teacher. Blended learning provides a path forward in education that values the teacher's role in blending technology and tradition. The success of blended learning hinges on the teacher's ability to skillfully select blended learning models and technology tools that meet specific learning objectives. This book is designed to help districts, schools, and leaders build a robust and sustainable professional learning infrastructure to support teachers as they shift to blended learning.

If you are picking up this book, I assume you do not need to be convinced of the merits of blended learning. For those who *do* need convincing, I've written two other books on the subject, *Blended Learning in Grades 4–12* and *Blended Learning in Action*. My first book, *Blended Learning in Grades 4–12*, supports individual teachers attempting to shift to a blended learning model. My second book, *Blended Learning in Action*, supports schools and districts making this shift by providing resources for teachers and leaders.

Schools are investing a lot of money into purchasing devices and building up their technology infrastructure, but few are investing equally to build a professional learning infrastructure. However, if schools do not develop a clear plan for supporting teachers as they shift to blended learning, then the financial investment in technology will not yield powerful shifts in teaching practices. Teachers need to continue learning if they are going to use technology to transform learning in their classrooms. This requires a commitment on the part of school leadership to prioritize professional learning and weave it into the fabric of the school.

This book presents a professional learning path for schools committed to blended learning. This path is not an easy one. It demands resources, dedication, and sacrifice. The reward is a school community working to blend technology and tradition to provide the most engaging learning experience possible for its students.

This book is written for school leaders and the coaches who work directly with teachers. Chapters 1–4 and Chapters 11–12 are written for *both* leadership and coaches and are identified by the following icon.

School Community Leaders & Coaches

Chapter 1 emphasizes articulating the *why* behind a shift to blended learning. Too often leaders begin by tackling the *what*. They make purchasing decisions about what technology to buy before they articulate the *why* driving the shift to blended learning. Leadership must articulate the *why* to get teachers on board with this shift.

Chapter 2 presents a roadmap for building a professional learning infrastructure. This roadmap will require that leadership make key decisions about how money is spent and how resources are allocated.

Chapter 3 reviews key elements of effective professional development and acknowledges the role an expert can play in helping to define the *why* and in unpacking the blended learning models so teachers understand their value. The expert can provide a spark, but the coaches and professional learning community are crucial to the long-term success of a shift to blended learning.

Chapter 4 defines the term *blended learning coach*, introduces the coaching cycle used in this book, and reviews the blended learning models.

Chapters 5–10 focus on providing blended learning coaches with concrete strategies and resources they can use to support teachers as they set goals, design blended lessons, implement blended learning models, and reflect on their practice. These chapters are identified by the following icon.

Chapter 11 focuses on the role virtual coaching can play in scaling high-quality coaching and connecting qualified coaches with teachers in various geographic locations.

Chapter 12 emphasizes the importance of gradually releasing professional learning to the teachers by building a professional learning community (PLC) in which teacher teams meet regularly to gather evidence, develop strategies, implement new strategies and models, analyze the impact of these strategies, and apply new knowledge.

Schoolwide change requires people at all levels—leadership, coaches, and teachers—to work together to define a clear vision and make that vision a reality. That's why this book is written with all three of these stakeholders in mind. In writing this book I've drawn heavily from my own work and experiences as a teacher, blended learning coach, and education consultant supporting districts as they shift to blended learning. I hope what I have learned will help support others as they navigate the changing landscape of education. It's time to invest in professional learning to support the shift to student-centered, student-paced learning environments that use technology strategically to place students at the center of learning.

Acknowledgments

AUTHOR'S ACKNOWLEDGMENTS

I want to thank the following educators for taking the time to share their thoughts on education, technology, and professional learning. I appreciate the work you do for teachers and students.

Mary Arnold

Anne Atherton

David Becker

Michelle Daml

Kyle Dunbar

Ivy Ewell-Eldridge

Matt Flugum

Jennifer Graham

Stacy Hawthorne

Tammy Hermance

Susan Horita

Jamay Johnson

Susan Johnson

Dominic Kirkpatrick

Mike Klein

Jenni LaBrie

Don Lourcey

Tosh McGaughy

Kathy Mason

Karen McKinley

Cheryl McKnight

Tracy Mulligan

Ashley Pacholewski

Mike Pothast

Deb Ramm

Clark Richardson

Lindsay Stephenson

Kathy Vergara

Sharon Wright

PUBLISHER'S ACKNOWLEDGMENTS

Corwin gratefully acknowledges the contributions of the following reviewers:

Sheila Fredericks, Technology Coordinator
The Concept School
Westtown, PA

Dr. Carol S. Holzberg, Director of Technology
Greenfield Public Schools
Greenfield, MA

Stephen Johnson, Curriculum Specialist—Technology
Panama-Buena Vista Union School District
Bakersfield, CA

Ruthanne Munger, Grade 5–8 Instructional Coach
Test Intermediate School
Richmond, IN

Brian Taylor, Director of Science and Engineering Technology K–12
West Islip UFSD
West Islip, NY

Melissa Wood-Glusac, TOHS English Teacher Grades 9–11
Thousand Oaks High School
Thousand Oaks, CA

About the Author

Catlin R. Tucker is a Google Certified Innovator, blended learning coach, bestselling author, international trainer, and keynote speaker who teaches in Sonoma County, where she was named Teacher of the Year in 2010. Catlin's books *Blended Learning in Grades 4–12* and *Blended Learning in Action* are both bestsellers. She has also written *Creatively Teach the Common Core Literacy Standards With Technology* to support teachers in thinking outside of the box as they shift to the Common Core. Catlin is working on her doctorate at Pepperdine University. She is active on Twitter @Catlin_Tucker and writes an internationally ranked education blog at CatlinTucker.com.

CHAPTER 1

School Community Leaders & Coaches

Articulate the WHY

The #1 barrier is mindset toward innovation—teachers must want to change their practice, especially when they have had some level of success in traditional classrooms. The greater the need for change, the more receptive teachers are to work differently. When the culture is ripe for innovation, the work can be accomplished. As long as teachers are satisfied with the status-quo, no amount of training and support will change practice.

—Cheryl McKnight (@cherylmkc),
digital learning coordinator

INTRODUCTION

There are many barriers to change in education. Change requires time, energy, and resources, all of which are in short supply at most schools. Our jobs are demanding and multifaceted. Teachers do not simply prepare and facilitate lessons. They attend meetings, communicate with parents, assess student work, meet students' emotional needs, and juggle the many district mandates that come their way. It's not surprising that most teachers feel they do not have the time or energy to experiment with new teaching strategies or technology tools.

When life gets tough, most people revert to what feels safe and familiar. Teachers are no different. When the demands of their profession feel daunting or overwhelming, most find comfort in doing what they have always done. In times of stress, venturing away from the familiar is scary and stressful. *Why try something new when what I am doing is working?* Unfortunately, just because something works does not mean it is working well or that it is the optimal way to go about a job or task.

This response has a biological underpinning. Research in neuroscience and experimental psychology is uncovering "evidence showing that different stress systems interact at different timescales to drive neural changes across the brain, bias attention, and shift reliance from a goal-directed, episodic memory system to a habit-based memory system" (Gagnon & Wagner, 2016, p. 55). The effect of acute stress on teacher and student learning has significant implications for education. When teachers experience acute stress stemming from the demands of their jobs, it makes it more challenging for them to move away from the habits they've cultivated over years and set and execute goals associated with a shift to something new and unfamiliar, like blended learning. In turn, students experience a similar response when navigating a teacher-controlled learning environment in which they have neither autonomy nor control.

When teachers are stuck in a place of fear, stress, and stagnation, it's the job of leadership to inspire teachers and create the sense of safety necessary to break free from the cycle of coping that perpetuates the status quo. When teachers feel safe and supported, they are more likely to adopt a mindset that sees change as positive and necessary.

This chapter will:

- Emphasize the importance of starting with *why* and articulating the purpose of a shift to blended learning

- Encourage leaders and teachers to work together to determine the *how* by identifying best practices for teaching and learning

- Help leaders and teachers identify *what* they want the student experience to be on campus

- Highlight the value of branding the shift to blended learning to generate excitement among stakeholders

- Introduce strategies for building a stronger school community that is ready to tackle change

WHY BLENDED LEARNING?

Michael Horn and Heather Staker (2014) defined blended learning as "any formal education program in which a student learns at least in part through online learning, with some element of student control over time, place, path and/or pace" (p. 34). When I work with teachers, I emphasize that *blended learning* is a big umbrella term that covers many different types of models, but the goal is to combine active, engaged learning online with active, engaged learning in the classroom to give students more control over those four elements of their learning.

> The goal of blended learning is to combine active, engaged learning online with active, engaged learning in the classroom to give students more control over those four elements of their learning.

In a traditional teacher-led, teacher-paced classroom, students do not have any control over time, place, path, or pace. Blended learning shifts control from the teacher to the student, allowing students to become drivers of their learning. This is a significant shift that requires teachers to rethink the way they design and facilitate lessons.

School leaders who want to inspire their teachers to take action and embrace blended learning must begin by articulating the *why*, as Simon Sinek (2009) asserted in his book *Start With Why*. Sinek said it is easy to articulate *what* people do, but it is much harder to articulate *why* people do what they do. Leaders must be crystal clear about the value of the change and make sure everyone within the organization understands the *why* driving the change. If leaders are clear about their *why*, teachers are more likely to buy in and take risks.

FIGURE 1.1 Simon Sinek's Golden Circle

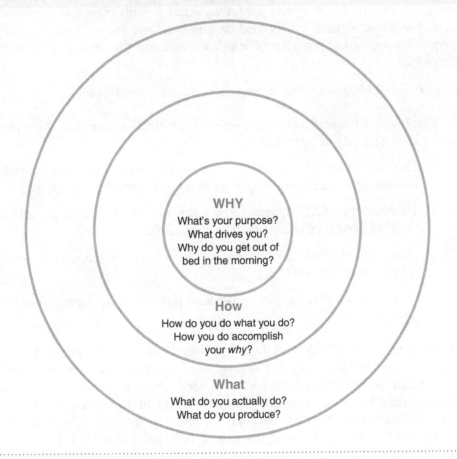

WHY
What's your purpose?
What drives you?
Why do you get out of
bed in the morning?

How
How do you do what you do?
How you do accomplish
your *why*?

What
What do you actually do?
What do you produce?

The *why* is an organization's purpose. And a clear sense of purpose is "the only way to maintain a lasting success and have a greater blend of innovation and flexibility" (Sinek, 2009, p. 50). Both are necessary to create meaningful change. When organizations—or, in this case, schools—are too focused on what they do instead of why they do it, change is harder to achieve because the purpose or value of the change is unclear.

Sinek talked about the Golden Circle, pictured in Figure 1.1 on the previous page, and stated that the most successful organizations work from the center outwards, defining their *why* first. Beginning with a clear statement of purpose or belief will drive the *how* and the *what*. Starting with *why* attracts people who share the same beliefs and values, making innovation and change easier to achieve. When members of an organization or community understand and believe in the same *why*, they are more likely to take risks and move beyond their own fear to make the *why* a reality.

I've worked with countless school districts that are embracing technology and blended learning models, but they do not communicate why this shift is important to teachers. The value proposition of the shift to blended learning is unclear. Without a clear sense of purpose, teachers become disillusioned and frustrated by the time and energy required to shift their teaching practices. Too often leaders are focused on the *how* and jump to logistics like large-scale technology purchases before articulating the *why* that's driving the change.

Leaders should begin by considering the following questions:

- How will blended learning improve the students' experience as learners or the quality of learning?

- How can blended learning spark curiosity, drive engagement, foster collaboration, and create opportunities to personalize learning?

- How will blended learning allow teachers to focus on the aspects of their job that they enjoy and find energizing?

- How can blended learning create more time for teachers to work directly with students?

- How will blended learning make learning more interesting, dynamic, and relevant?

If leaders take time to reflect on these questions at the start of a blended learning initiative, they will have a clearer sense of the *why* that is driving a shift from traditional teaching methods to blended learning. Articulating a clear purpose may be easier to accomplish if teachers understand how blended learning is different from a traditional approach to teaching. The shift from traditional teaching to blended learning is reflected in Figure 1.2, which is adapted from an iNACOL report by Chris Sturgis.

FIGURE 1.2 Shifting Mindsets

TRADITIONAL TEACHING	BLENDED LEARNING
Teacher-led, teacher-paced instruction	Student-centered, student-paced learning
One size fits all	Personalization
Teacher-controlled learning environments	Flexible learning environments
Focus on compliance	Focus on collaboration
Work characterized by conformity	Work characterized by creativity
Traditional cumulative grading system	Data-driven, competency-based learning

Source: Adapted from iNACOL report.

The Blended Learning Teacher Competency Framework, a report published by iNACOL in 2014, defined *mindsets* as "core values or beliefs that guide thinking, behaviors and actions that align with goals of educational change" (Powell, Rabbitt, & Kennedy, p. 10). School leadership must align teachers' core values and beliefs with the goals associated with a shift to blended learning. This requires that leadership get teachers on board with the purpose behind this shift, making it clear how teachers' values are in line with the goals of blended learning.

GETTING TEACHERS ON BOARD WITH THE WHY

The *why* that drives an organization is anchored in the organization's beliefs and values. Members of an organization will support a vision if they feel it is in line with their own beliefs and values. Sinek (2009) pointed out that "we trust those with whom we are able to perceive common values or beliefs" (p. 53), so leadership must play a central role in highlighting the commonality between the beliefs and values held by members in the organization.

School leaders should dedicate time to an activity designed to surface the staff's shared values and then clearly connect these values to the *why* behind the shift to blended learning. This is best done at the start of a school year, which is typically a time of optimism and excitement. I'd suggest school leaders use this high-energy time to engage the staff in a conversation about what they value. This is a great way to get teachers talking about why they teach and what motivates them.

Creating buy-in and generating support is especially important when we are asking people to adopt new mindsets, take risks, and move outside of their comfort zones, as is the case when educators are tasked with shifting to blended learning. Once the *why* is clear, then it's time to move on to the *how*. What will teachers actually do to achieve the *why*?

"WHAT WE VALUE"
Word Cloud Activity

1. Encourage your teachers to form small groups and take turns answering the following questions:

   a. What are you most looking forward to this year?

   b. Why do you teach? What motivates you to do this job?

   c. What is important about your work? What do you value in education?

   d. What does student success look like? What does teacher success look like?

   e. Is there something new you plan to try this year?

   f. If you could plan our next professional development day, what would you like to learn?

2. After the discussion, ask your teachers to take a couple of minutes to identify three things they value in relation to their work. Encourage them to start with the phrase "I value . . ." and complete it.

3. Use technology to create transparency. I'd suggest using Mentimeter, which allows the user to pose a question and then collect responses in a word cloud format that updates in real time as people submit their responses. Words that are repeated by multiple people will appear larger, easily highlighting shared core values. Once the word cloud has been created, leave it projected so everyone can see it for the follow-up discussion.

4. Break teachers into small groups and give them time to discuss the following questions:

   a. What words in the word cloud are really big and signal a shared core value? What do the largest words reveal about our shared beliefs? How are these values visible in our school right now?

   b. What can we do as staff to make our values clear to students, parents, and other school stakeholders?

   c. Are there any words missing from the word cloud that you would have expected to see? Did you expect any of the smaller words to appear larger?

   d. Given the values identified, what would you expect to see in a classroom? What changes might bring our campus into closer alignment with our values? How might a shift to blended learning help us to bring our teaching more in line with our values?

THE **HOW**: BEST PRACTICES

Once a school has articulated its core values, it's crucial to explain what those values look like in practice. It's easy to state what we value but harder to pin down what those values look like in a classroom and on a campus. However, if teachers and coaches take time to describe what teaching and learning *should* look like, this makes clear what all members of the school community are striving for. It also makes it easier for coaches to provide teachers meaningful feedback during observations and real-time coaching sessions to ensure teaching and learning are in line with best practices. Consider the following questions as you think about best practices (the *how*):

- What would we want a person visiting our school to see if he or she entered a random classroom?
- What does the classroom environment look like?
- What are students doing?
- What is the teacher doing?
- How is technology being used?

Windsor High School, where I have taught for 15 years, states that one of its core values is that "learning takes place when students and staff are actively engaged in the learning process." Given that this is a core value, visitors should expect to see students asking questions, problem solving, and collaborating. However, if students are seated in rows listening to a teacher lecture for large chunks of time, then there is clearly a disconnect between the stated core value of active, engaged learning and the teaching practice. Any disconnect between the stated core values and the actual experience in the classroom leads to a loss of credibility and authenticity.

Think about the core values identified in the "What We Value" Word Cloud Activity, then for each core value state what it looks like in terms of the *teaching* happening in the classroom and what it looks like in terms of the *learning* happening in the classroom.

- What will teachers do to ensure each core value is evident in their teaching practice?
- What will students do to ensure each core value is evident in their learning?

These are tough questions to answer and may require some time, discussion, and fine-tuning. However, they should ultimately make it clear what a random visitor to a classroom can expect to see. Clearly stating behaviors that characterize best practices for teaching and learning makes it clear which concrete behaviors schools are attempting to employ and, ultimately, master.

I'd love for schools to approach the formation of their one-page WHY document, pictured in Figure 1.3, the same way the International Society for Technology in Education (ISTE) went about updating its student standards in 2016. ISTE engaged its members and stakeholders in conversations about what should be included in the standards, then it published a working draft via Google Document with an open invitation for stakeholders and community members to explore, comment on, and suggest changes and improvements to the student standards prior to the final draft being published. By making the working draft viewable and open to comment and revision, ISTE invited people in the education and technology worlds to engage in the process. As a result, the final draft was stronger and represented the range of technology skills students today need to be successful beyond high school.

FIGURE 1.3 WHY Document Template

WHY

What is the purpose of the shift to blended learning?

HOW

How will best practices for learning and teaching help you achieve your why?

How will students ensure each core value is evident in their learning?	How will teachers ensure each core value is evident in their teaching practice?

WHAT

What will the student experience on your campus be like?

online resources Available for download at bit.ly/WhyBlended.

A public declaration of shared values has a unifying effect on a staff. In his book *Unmistakable Impact*, Jim Knight (2011a) pointed out that in a school "committed to dramatically improving professional learning, everyone in the school must have a clear understanding of the goal and how to get there" (p. 9). He argued that most school improvement plans are too dense, lengthy, and convoluted to be effective guides for change. Instead, he emphasized the importance of a simple plan with clear goals. He suggested creating a one-page plan that "clearly describes critical teaching behaviors" (2011a, p. 56). A one-page WHY document can serve this purpose beautifully.

If your school uses the template above to draft your school's *why* (purpose), *how* (best practices), and *what* (student experience) for teaching and learning, then it can be published online for staff, students, parents, and community members to read, think about, and critique. This way everyone has a voice in the formation of this important document before it is shared with the larger community.

THE **WHAT**: BRANDING THE SHIFT TO BLENDED LEARNING

Many of your teachers, students, parents, and community members may not know what blended learning means or why it's worth investing time, energy, and resources into this shift. Building a brand around your shift to blended learning can generate interest and support.

Branding is a strategy organizations use to build an identity that is recognizable to others. Branding explains who an organization is and what it wants to accomplish. It can also serve to create a narrative about the organization that's compelling. This narrative can help to motivate the people within the organization and attract interest and support from the larger community. Because blended learning is a departure from the status quo, many parents may not understand the benefits of a shift away from traditional instruction. Branding can get parents and community members on board with and excited about change. It can make them feel as though they are part of something special and progressive.

> Branding can get parents and community members on board with and excited about change. It can make them feel as though they are part of something special and progressive.

As schools vie for students and the funding that comes with them, building a strong brand around blended learning that is appealing to the community is important. According to *Fortune*, in 2017 Google became the most valuable brand in the world, with an estimated worth of $109.5 billion (Farber, 2017). Google knows that its brand shapes how customers perceive the company.

As schools evolve and embrace new approaches to teaching and learning, it's crucial that they too build a brand, or identity, that's recognizable in the community. This brand will help people unfamiliar with blended learning better understand what the school is doing and why. It will paint a picture of what a student's experience at that school will be.

> *The pace of change is slow in most classrooms. This is because many teachers need time to understand the technology and how to integrate it effectively in their classrooms. This is hard for me on a personal level because every additional day it takes a teacher to adjust means that 30–150 students were denied an opportunity to learn content in a way that is tailored to their learning needs. Sometimes we focus so heavily on the adults in the edtech equation that we miss the important factor—students and their learning.*
>
> **—Stacy Hawthorne (@StacyHaw), Online Programs Director for the Davidson Academy and experienced educational strategist**

Thorne (2003) pointed out that "'branding' an organization means focusing on the key components and encouraging consistency across all functions" (p. 7). By establishing a brand as an organization, it's easier to get all stakeholders on the same page in terms of understanding their shared purpose and goals. Branding also forces an organization to focus on the customers and put them at the center or "heart of the organization" and to "[build] everything else around them" (Thorne, 2003, p. 7). Imagine if schools did this! Our customers are our students. If we focused on what would best serve *them* instead of getting bogged down by other details, this would have a radical impact on the way we articulate our purpose and goals.

Although a school may have a clear mission statement that is prominently displayed on its website, that statement is different from a brand promise. A *mission statement* is designed for internal use to inspire and motivate employees at a company. By contrast, a *brand promise* is designed for external use to articulate an experience customers can expect from that company. It is the brand promise that needs to be articulated and posted on a school website. Figure 1.4 provides a side-by-side comparison of a mission statement versus a brand promise.

FIGURE 1.4 Mission Statement Versus Brand Promise

MISSION STATEMENT	BRAND PROMISE
Google's mission is to organize the world's information and make it universally accessible and useful.	*Google's brand promise is to be the world's number one source of information.*
Internal	External
Designed to motivate and inspire employees	Designed to help others understand who you are and what you do
Articulates a clear purpose for employees	Articulates an experience customers can expect
Connects employees to your specific organization	Connects consumers to your specific organization

The process of building a brand and articulating a brand promise can help an organization to better understand its own purpose. Ultimately, branding can shape the development of culture, because as author and branding expert Nick Westergaard (2013) explained, "At its core, your brand promise should define your entire business and should touch every aspect of your company." If an organization is committed to its stated brand promise, then its values, norms, language, and habits will all function to support that promise and, in effect, cultivate a culture in line with it. According to Westergaard, the best way to articulate a clear brand is by following a simple formula: "What you do for whom." As schools think about branding their shift to blended learning, they must answer these two questions:

- What do we do?
- For whom do we do it?

These two simple questions can guide an organization to a brand that articulates what the customers—in our case, students—can expect from the organization or school. In his article "The 5 Building Blocks of an Effective Brand Promise," Marcus Varner (2017) emphasized that an effective brand promise must be simple, credible, different, memorable, and inspiring. As schools begin to articulate and refine their brand promise, it's key to keep these five criteria in mind.

If the leadership team heading the conversation about branding the shift to blended learning needs inspiration, it's worth taking time to explore some of the brand promises made by the most successful companies to get a sense of how they articulate what they do and for whom they do it. Starbucks' brand promise is "to inspire and nurture the human spirit—one person, one cup, and one community at a time." Nike's brand promise is "to bring inspiration and innovation to every athlete* in the world." You'll notice these are powerful statements, not lengthy paragraphs. The brand promise must be short and unique enough to be instantly recognizable to staff, students, parents, and community members.

Ultimately, a school's brand promise articulates an experience that students will have on a campus, but it does not require that every teacher teach the exact same way. As schools go through the process of conveying a brand promise, school leaders must make it clear that each classroom is a unique space striving to fulfill this promise. That autonomy, freedom, and creativity are essential for teachers to stay motivated and inspired.

EIGHT WAYS TO STRENGTHEN YOUR SCHOOL COMMUNITY

Articulating the *why, how*, and *what* will create a foundation upon which to build as you transition to blended learning. It will also keep the school focused on what's important when the transition gets rocky. If teachers are to be inspired and willing to take risks, they need to feel safe and supported.

---

*According to Nike co-founder Bill Bowerman, "If you have a body, you are an athlete."

They must believe it is okay to fail and that failing is simply part of learning. The stronger the school community, the more comfortable teachers will feel taking risks and failing as they work to adopt various blended learning models and navigate new technology.

Tight-knit families tend to have several things in common. They make time to eat, talk, and play together. Some of the most successful and progressive companies, such as Google and Netflix, also take cues from families to build strong bonds between employees and motivate them to do their best work. Both Google and Netflix cater healthy meals for their staff, and the Google complex has a volleyball court and "play" areas for employees to take brain breaks and connect with colleagues.

School communities could learn a lot from families and progressive companies when it comes to concrete strategies designed to build relationships among teachers and cultivate a positive school culture, which is critical to change. The importance of relationship building cannot be overstated. Change is scary, but it's a lot less scary when you are surrounded by people you feel connected to and supported by, so here are some strategies for building a strong school community.

1. Start the Year With a Staff Retreat

Most teachers begin their school year in nuts-and-bolts meetings. These meetings cover a range of topics, but they rarely inspire or provide opportunities for educators to get to know one another. A staff retreat, by contrast, creates the time and space to build relationships; establish (or revisit) your brand promise, core values, and best teaching and learning practices; and play to learn.

In the first few years of my teaching career at Windsor High School, we had a 48-hour staff retreat. These 2 days were dedicated to team building, collaborating, sharing meals, and sitting around a campfire at night talking. There was something really special about these retreats. I felt a little like a kid at camp making new friends. We should all have those moments with our colleagues to build trust and form meaningful relationships.

2. Start a Breakfast Club or Organize Staff Lunches

Too often teachers, myself included, don't leave their classrooms during lunch. This adds to the feeling that we work in silos and are disconnected from our colleagues. It may be unrealistic to think teachers can eat a meal together every day, but it's worth making shared meals a priority. It's no accident that most families who eat dinner together every night report having stronger relationships with one another. Sharing a meal and engaging in informal conversations brings people together.

Michael Cox, an educator I connected with on Twitter, shared that his school started their own "Breakfast Club," with various departments hosting a breakfast one Friday each month. These breakfasts are inclusive of everyone, and teachers, support staff, custodians, and administration are all invited to connect.

If your school is organized into quads or buildings, ask each section of the campus to sign up to host a potluck. It could be a weekly event (e.g., Fun Friday) or a monthly event (e.g., First Friday of the Month). The regularity of a staff lunch may depend on the size of the campus, but it's worth instituting a regular meal together. I remember working with the staff at Robert Louis Stevenson Middle School in St. Helena, California, and they took turns preparing lunch for each other each Friday. It was clearly a cherished routine they all enjoyed. They spent that weekly lunch catching up, sharing stories, and brainstorming project ideas. It's no coincidence they're one of the most collegial staffs I've ever worked with.

3. Break the Ice and Have Fun

People are constantly joining and leaving a school community. Teachers retire, take leaves of absence, and get hired mid-year, which means there should always be opportunities for teachers to make connections with one another. Beginning every staff meeting with a fun icebreaker activity can encourage teachers to connect and learn one another's names.

4. Share Best Teaching Practices

Schools prioritize sharing student work at open houses and expositions, but teacher work is rarely highlighted and celebrated. Schools should make time to share best teaching practices. Invite teachers to share their best lessons, project ideas, and classroom routines with staff in a campus bulletin, during department time, or at the end of each staff meeting.

5. Create a Snaps Jar

"Snap" is teenager speak for something close to "wow" + "nice job" + "I'm impressed," so create a snap jar in the staff room to encourage colleagues on a campus to recognize one another's innovation and hard work.

On my campus, our vice principal set out a big glass jar with colorful cards next to it. The staff is encouraged to write notes to their colleagues praising the work they are doing and/or thanking them for something inspiring or supportive they've done. Those cards find their way into our boxes at the end of each month. It's an easy way to recognize the talents of the wonderful people we work with.

6. Begin a Book Study

Staff members who learn together, grow together. Start a staff book club or initiate a staff-wide book study of a text such as *Drive, Most Likely to Succeed,*

Visible Learning for Teachers, or *Blended Learning in Action* to get teachers thinking about and discussing topics ranging from human motivation to different approaches to teaching and learning.

7. Host Unconferences

The unconference model is an easy way for teachers to informally share best practices. Instead of an administrative meeting, bring teachers together and give everyone a sticky note. Ask them to identify a teaching strategy, technology tool, or other classroom tip they would enjoy sharing with their colleagues and write it on the sticky note. Display the sticky notes and ask teachers to put a dot on the three sticky notes they are most interested in. The sticky notes with the most dots will be the topics of the unconference. Teachers can host a short session in their classrooms or simply lead a conversation in the space where the all-staff administrative meeting takes place (e.g., library). When administrators replace a handful of admin meetings each year with unconference-style sharing sessions, they send a clear message that they value their teachers' knowledge and the process of learning from one another.

8. Wednesday Walks

Wednesday Walks encourage teachers to get out of their rooms during their prep period and walk into another classroom to see what that teacher is doing in his or her room. Too often teachers feel like they teach in isolation. Wednesday Walks break down those walls and invite teachers to learn from the work happening all around them.

By dedicating one day each week to walking through another classroom, teachers are inspired to plan dynamic lessons on Wednesdays because they know they will have colleagues coming into their rooms. It also gets teachers out of their rooms to be inspired. These walks are informal and can be as long or short as a teacher wants.

There are a multitude of strategies school leaders can use to build community and camaraderie on campus to ensure teachers feel respected, valued, supported, and inspired. This will translate into a community willing to take risks together and learn from one another and willing to celebrate each other's successes and rally around those who fail. This is the culture schools must cultivate if they want to prioritize learning and innovation.

Knowing your *why* and having a strong sense of community are requirements for implementing a successful blended learning initiative. In the next chapter, we'll explore the roadmap for building a professional learning infrastructure to support sustainable change.

BOOK STUDY QUESTIONS

1. In general, how comfortable are your teachers when it comes to trying something new? Are teachers excited about or resistant to using technology? Do you think your teachers feel safe failing at your school?

2. Look closely at the core values articulated by the Urban School of San Francisco (www.urbanschool.org) and discuss what you notice about them. How are they similar to or different from your school's core values? What do they reflect about the Urban School?

3. What is the *why* driving your shift to blended learning? Look at the questions on page 6 and consider what your answers reveal about your *why*.

4. How can you engage stakeholders in the process of articulating and refining your *why*, *how*, and *what*? Who should lead this process? What might that process look like? Would you invite asynchronous online dialogue using a working document or physically bring people together to discuss it?

5. How can you engage teachers in a conversation about the *how* (best practices)? How can this conversation be used to bring teachers together and foster collaboration?

6. How are you currently building a positive school culture? Do you use any of the strategies suggested in this chapter? If so, have they been successful? If not, which of these strategies would work to build community on your campus? What would you add to this list?

CHAPTER 2

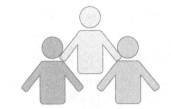

School Community Leaders & Coaches

A Roadmap for Building a Professional Learning Infrastructure

Many teachers have never even seen a classroom where the technology is being utilized to truly meet every student where they are at and help push them forward; it is almost hard for them to imagine a classroom that functions that way.

—Clark Richardson (@cdrich86),
technology integration specialist

INTRODUCTION

Blended learning seeks to shift the classroom from a teacher-focused and teacher-paced learning environment to a student-centered space where learners have some control over the time, place, pace, and path of their learning. Professional development should mirror this shift in the realm of professional learning. Instead of periodic all-staff training sessions that often follow a "sit and get" model, professional development focused on blended learning should combine targeted training, one-on-one coaching, and professional learning communities (PLCs) to place the focus on the learners—in this case, the teachers—to ensure they feel supported as they learn about blended learning models, teaching strategies, and technology tools.

To effectively support teachers transitioning to a blended model, schools must reimagine their approach to professional learning. Instead of a handful of professional development days, professional learning must be built into the school schedule so it's ongoing, relevant, and effective.

This chapter will:

- Define the scope of professional learning as it relates to this book
- Share a simple yet effective strategy for training teachers in a whole group setting
- Introduce the one-on-one coaching cycle
- Describe the purpose a professional learning community fulfills for a long-term professional learning strategy

BLENDED LEARNING DEMANDS A NEW APPROACH TO PROFESSIONAL LEARNING

The impact of technology on the way we learn and engage with the world demands that educators integrate technology seamlessly into their teaching practice to ensure students learn important life skills in conjunction with the subject matter. In my last book, *Blended Learning in Action* (Tucker, Wycoff, & Green, 2016), I wrote that when blended learning is implemented successfully, it enables the following hallmarks of best teaching and learning practices:

- **Personalization:** providing unique learning pathways for individual students
- **Agency:** giving learners opportunities to participate in key decisions
- **Authentic audience:** giving learners opportunities to create for a real audience both locally and globally
- **Connectivity:** providing learners opportunities to learn collaboratively with peers and experts both locally and globally
- **Creativity:** providing learners individual and collaborative opportunities to make things that matter

To reach these hallmarks of best teaching and learning practices, teachers both aspiring and current have to understand and appreciate the value of technology for both increasing student academic success and improving teacher effectiveness. However, a 2013 report titled *Learning in the 21st Century*, which was based on data collected by education nonprofit Project Tomorrow, revealed some stark differences in the way aspiring educators view technology's role in education compared to current classroom teachers. Fifty-one percent of current classroom teachers believe technology can make lessons more interactive, 37% feel that technology could allow for more student-centered learning, 38% think technology can help them to create more relevant lessons, and only 23% feel that technology could increase the connection between teacher and students (Project Tomorrow, 2013).

This data suggests that teachers both aspiring and current need a better understanding of how technology can make lessons more engaging by placing students at the center of learning in the classroom. Training must focus on technology's ability to spark student creativity, allow for student ownership over their learning, and foster collaboration. However, using technology in the classroom is a daunting task for many teachers who lack the time, support, and confidence to experiment. It's critical that school districts rethink their approach to professional development and weave professional learning into the fabric of the school day to provide ongoing learning opportunities for teachers. Learning cannot be isolated to a few staff development days each school year.

So how do we bridge the gap and get all educators to recognize the value of technology? How do we help teachers see that technology, when used effectively, has the potential to positively impact student academic success and teacher effectiveness? The short answer is professional learning. This book strives to provide a more in-depth answer to the challenge of scaling high-quality professional learning.

PROFESSIONAL DEVELOPMENT: DEFINING THE SCOPE

Professional development is an umbrella term that encompasses a wide range of learning activities aimed at helping professionals in the field of education continue learning and honing their skills. Because this definition is so broad, educators will hear *professional development* (PD) used to describe a wide array of learning opportunities, including workshops, all-staff training sessions, conferences, online courses, peer coaching, advanced degree programs, and more. In addition to these more formal approaches to professional learning, there are also informal ways that teachers learn, as pictured in Figure 2.1 on the next page. Informal learning is as valuable as formal learning because it is teacher driven. It may include engaging in conversations with colleagues about teaching strategies, watching YouTube videos, writing and reading blogs, or connecting with other educators via social media.

Professional development can be facilitated by outside experts and consultants, on-site teachers or administrators, staff from the district office, coaches, or outside organizations. Professional development can span a single day or be embedded into a teacher's schedule. Some professional development is required by the school, while other forms of it are optional.

So, the type of learning, length of learning, and person leading the learning can be wildly different depending on a person's interpretation of the term *professional development*. This broad definition can muddy the conversation about what effective professional development looks like for teachers, administrators, and other credentialed staff on a school campus. For the purpose of this book, I'm narrowing the scope of the conversation to the following three types of professional learning:

1. Targeted training led by experts or trainers

2. One-on-one coaching

3. Participation in a PLC that includes ongoing, non-evaluative peer coaching

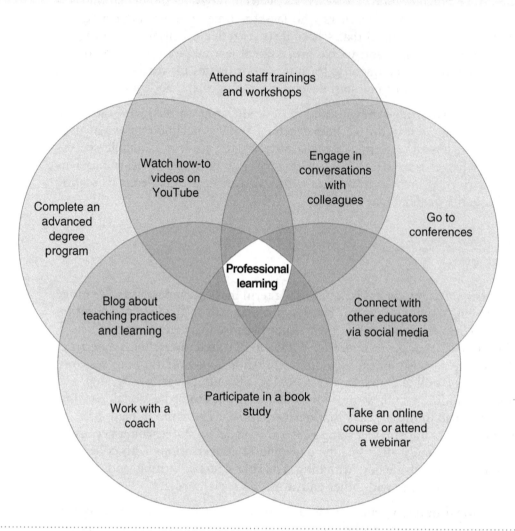

Attend staff trainings and workshops

Watch how-to videos on YouTube

Engage in conversations with colleagues

Complete an advanced degree program

Go to conferences

Professional learning

Blog about teaching practices and learning

Connect with other educators via social media

Work with a coach

Participate in a book study

Take an online course or attend a webinar

I've chosen these three specific types of professional learning because they allow for a gradual release of learning to educators over time, as pictured in Figure 2.2. Instead of treating professional learning as an event with a beginning and end, it must be embedded into the design of the school.

The Spark: Establish the WHY

Professional learning that follows a gradual release model should begin with a "spark" that hooks your teachers and gains their buy-in. Typically, an expert is brought into a school to establish the *why*, or the purpose of a shift to blended learning. I play this role for school districts frequently. I come in for 1 or 2 days of intensive blended learning training to articulate the value

FIGURE 2.2 Gradual Release of Professional Learning to Educators

Spark
Training with an expert to understand the WHY behind a shift to blended learning

Coaching
One-on-one work with a coach to learn the HOW of blended learning

PLCs
Collaborative teams refine and improve what they do

of blended learning, provide a long-term vision for change, and get teachers excited about blended learning. It's important for teachers to see the value in the change, and that is something a dynamic presenter with expertise in the field can help facilitate effectively.

During this first stage, it is important to keep the scope of the training narrow to allow time for the expert to actively engage teachers in hands-on, practice-based work. Chapter 3 identifies a simple training approach experts can use to ensure these larger group training sessions provide a foundation on which the coaches and PLCs can build. If an expert does not actively engage participants, teachers are unlikely to walk away from the training willing and able to implement new strategies and use new forms of technology. The most effective whole group training sessions will also employ the strategies that school leaders want teachers to use after the training.

Blended Learning Coaches: Support the HOW

Following a whole group training session, blended learning coaches must take the information presented in the training and help the teachers figure out how to apply what they learned in their classrooms. Given the high ratio of teachers to coaches, it's most manageable to begin coaching teachers who are either leading a blended learning pilot or teachers who are early adopters. For the purposes of this book, I'll refer to these early adopters as *teacher trailblazers*. These folks are key to creating change on a campus.

Peter Senge identified innovative educators as a primary leverage for change in school and stated, "We must unleash the forces of innovation and passion of individuals" (as quoted in Sparks, 2001, p. 43). It's ideal to identify and support these innovative teacher trailblazers early in a shift to blended learning because they will embrace change and serve as models for other teachers who are more hesitant to try new teaching strategies. The coaching phase provides these pilot teachers and teacher trailblazers with consistent support and feedback as they implement new teaching techniques and blended learning models.

Professional Learning Communities: Develop and Refine the WHAT

Finally, teachers must be organized in PLCs and given dedicated time in their schedules to meet and use the various parts of the coaching cycle to provide one another with ongoing support and non-evaluative feedback. In this final step, the teachers own the professional learning and work collaboratively to ensure they continue learning and evolving as a group.

These three interconnected elements of professional development—targeted training with an expert, one-on-one coaching, and PLCs—should be part of a school's strategic plan to help educators shift to blended learning. However, it requires that leaders rethink the master schedule, use of facilities, goals of professional development, and budget priorities.

Even though I will be focusing on training, coaching, and PLCs, it's important to acknowledge how valuable it is for educators to pursue their own learning and interests by attending conferences, signing up for online courses, and connecting with other educators on social media to supplement these three types of learning. The more educators aggressively pursue their own learning, the more excited they will be to try new teaching strategies and technology tools.

THE SPARK: ON-SITE TARGETED TRAINING LED BY AN EXPERT

Everyone needs to be inspired. It's easy to become disillusioned with our profession. I've had moments during my career where I've thought, "I've made an enormous mistake becoming a teacher. This is not what I signed up for!" Most educators experience these moments, which is why powerful professional development with an expert can be inspiring and rejuvenating. Any school or district trying to excite teachers to make a significant change in their approach to teaching should organize an event aimed at energizing teachers while also articulating *why* this shift is worth the time, energy, and effort. I call this moment "the spark."

The spark is just the beginning of a larger movement aimed at supporting teachers. Too often, school districts plan a handful of professional development days over the course of the year and the learning ends there. Teachers do not have support as they consider how to implement new strategies in their classrooms. If a physical education teacher or choir teacher goes to a training session on a specific blended learning model, he or she may leave intrigued but is going to need support to figure out how to apply those strategies to his or her particular teaching assignments. If the professional development training is a stand-alone event, the spark will fizzle and teachers will revert to what is comfortable.

To turn the spark into a flame, single-day training sessions with an expert must be followed by coaching. Ideally, coaches work one-on-one with an educator to take a new strategy and figure out what it will look like in that educator's classroom. If a training session is not tailored to a teacher's specific grade level or subject area, which is often the case, then it's the coach's job to bridge that gap and help the teacher apply the strategy in the context of his or her teaching assignment.

ONE-ON-ONE COACHING

The value of a coach's role in continued learning and development makes intuitive sense, but a coach also plays a pivotal role in supporting the coachee through moments of doubt and failure. For those of us who enjoy sports, we know that even athletes at the highest levels of competition have coaches who they credit with their development as players. Many athletes also touch on the important role their coaches play as mentors, providing a safe space for the athlete to practice and fail. For example, in an interview with Simon Briggs (2016) for *The Telegraph*, Andy Murray, arguably one of the best tennis players in the world, said, "Ivan [Lendl] is the best coach I've had. It was good to have someone who could normalise failing." This quote speaks to the reality that everyone who is working to develop a skill needs a support system. We all need to feel it is okay to fail and that our failures are a necessary part of learning. A coach plays this key role in professional learning.

The coach cannot be the expert on everything, especially when it comes to the ever-changing landscape of technology, which is why targeted professional development in the form of single-day or multiday training with an expert is valuable to introduce both the coaches and the teachers to new strategies and tools. After the initial spark is ignited by an expert, the coaches and PLCs on a campus must act as the long-term support network for teachers.

Coaching is identified by Joyce and Showers (2002) as the most effective factor in professional learning; however, most professional development still occurs in a single day. This approach to professional development fails to build in the necessary time to allow teachers to discuss strategies, practice strategies in a simulated environment with other teachers, and reflect on the best way to use a chosen strategy with their students. Building these key elements into all training sessions, whether small group or whole staff, is an important *first* step in supporting the shift to blended learning. Chapter 3 explores how to make the most of training sessions led by an expert or trainer.

In this book I will introduce a coaching cycle that supports teachers from the early stages of goal setting and lesson planning to teaching and reflecting. The specific coaching cycle described in this book (and pictured in Figure 2.3) includes (1) initial conversation and goal setting, (2) initial observation and debrief, (3) co-lesson planning, (4) real-time coaching, (5) model lessons and co-teaching, and (6) documenting, reflecting, and revisiting goals.

Depending on a teacher's progress and needs, a coach can repeat steps as many times as necessary. I've spent several sessions lesson planning with teachers who struggle to conceptualize a blended lesson that does not follow a linear whole group agenda. Other teachers feel confident lesson planning after only one session and prefer to plan on their own and share their lessons with me via Google Docs for feedback. Similarly, some teachers feel more comfortable trying something new if I am there to co-teach, so I spend time in their classrooms leading a station or lending support as students navigate a blended lesson. The coaching cycle is flexible, and progress through the steps can be customized for individual teachers.

Chapters 5–10 will focus on each step of the coaching cycle and explain how coaches can maximize the effectiveness of coaching by leveraging technology. Each step in the coaching cycle plays an important role in developing trust between coach and teacher as well as in supporting the teacher in designing, implementing, and reflecting on her or his blended learning journey.

PROFESSIONAL LEARNING COMMUNITIES (PLCs)

Professional learning communities (PLCs) are designed to transform schools into learning communities where teachers are connected to develop and share knowledge. They are a "vehicle for establishing collegial relationships and for building capacity for change within a school" (Blankenship & Ruona,

FIGURE 2.3 Blended Learning Coaching Cycle

Blended Learning Coaching Cycle ⟹

1. Initial Conversation and Goal Setting

Coach outlines his/her role in this process. Then coach and teacher identify their goals for using blended learning models and technology.

2. Initial Observation and Debrief

Coach observes a lesson and takes notes. Then coach and teacher debrief.

6. Documenting, Reflecting, and Revisiting Goals

Coach and teacher review documentation, data, and initial goals to reflect on what worked and what needs to be refined and improved.

5. Model Lessons and Co-teaching

As the teacher employs new blended learning models, like Station Rotation, or uses a new technology tool, the coach acts as a co-teacher to lead parts of the lesson.

4. Real-time Coaching

As teacher facilitates a lesson, the coach is there to provide real-time suggestions and modifications by pressing "pause" on a lesson.

3. Co-lesson Planning

Coach and teacher work collaboratively to design a lesson that employs a blended learning model and uses technology strategically.

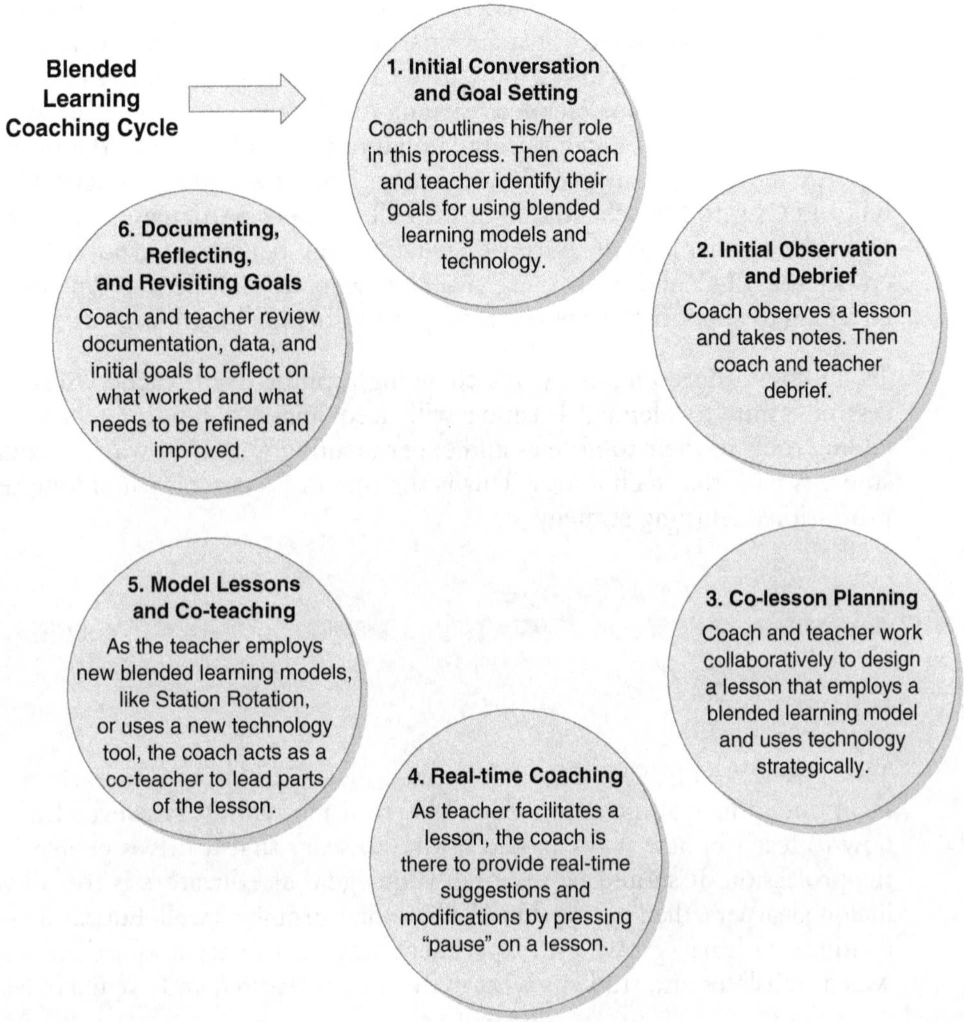

2007). Given how rapidly technology is changing the landscape of learning, it's imperative that schools have a long-term strategy for developing and sharing knowledge. Teachers can no longer afford to teach and learn in isolation. For schools to meet the myriad challenges they face, teachers must work in collaborative teams to identify challenges, design solutions, collect data, and reflect on their practice together. Teachers often feel they work in silos and rarely have time to meet with their peers to discuss their teaching practices. The goal of a PLC is to facilitate professional dialogue and continue the learning on a campus through inquiry and action. PLCs create time and space for colleagues to collaborate and learn from one another.

Due to scheduling challenges, some schools make participation in teacher teams voluntary, while at other schools participation is a requirement and time to meet is built into the master schedule. When participation in a PLC is voluntary, the percentage of teachers participating tends to be low and those who opt in are typically more motivated to keep learning. Those eager teachers are likely to be your blended learning trailblazers, so it's helpful to have them lead change on a campus and collaborate regularly with the teachers who are more reluctant to embrace change. This is why it's more effective to build PLCs into the schedule to ensure all teachers participate. Chapter 12 will delve further into the purpose, structure, and benefits of grouping teachers in the PLC and leveraging teachers who've experienced one-on-one coaching to support their peers in the shift to blended learning.

Technology isn't going away. It's changing rapidly. Even teachers who successfully shift to blended learning will need ongoing support to continue adding tools to their toolboxes and experimenting with new ways to engage students with that technology. This is the role PLCs can play in a long-term professional learning strategy.

WRAP UP

The tidal wave of technology has pushed many educators into early retirement due to fear of having to learn how to teach with it. However, learning how to teach in new ways should not be so scary that it drives people from the profession. It should be exciting. If our goal as educators is to cultivate lifelong learners, then we must model lifelong learning as well. Educators who continue to learn, grow, and experiment stay passionate about their work, which translates into students who, in turn, are interested and excited to learn.

Unfortunately, many teachers resent being asked to change because they don't feel supported. They may already be frustrated by large class sizes, lack of access to resources, pressure to teach specific standards, or too many new initiatives introduced without the necessary follow-through. Teachers face myriad challenges that drain their energy and cause them to push back when asked to make significant changes. So leadership must think about how it can cultivate a culture that values and prioritizes a professional learning infrastructure that offers teachers long-term support as they make fundamental changes to their teaching.

The most effective way to produce long-term, sustainable change is to offer ongoing support, feedback, and learning opportunities in the form of targeted training; on-site, one-on-one coaching; and participation in PLCs. This model is particularly effective because it personalizes professional development, allowing colleagues to work together to improve their practice all year long.

BOOK STUDY QUESTIONS

1. What types of professional learning do your teachers typically experience in a school year? Do you bring experts on-site to train teachers? Do you encourage teachers to attend conferences to learn?

2. How much training is offered to teachers each school year? Does your school have a set number of professional development days used for training? Is there any ongoing training available to teachers? Is there a way to build more informal training opportunities into your current schedule?

3. Who typically leads training sessions? Are trainers usually hired from outside of the district? Are there people on campus (e.g., instructional coaches) who are responsible for developing whole staff and small group training sessions? How successful have those sessions been? How do you measure the success of a training session (e.g., teacher ratings, percentage of teachers implementing new strategies or technology tools)?

4. How do you identify the topics or skills that will be the focus of the training sessions you organize? How do you engage your teachers' voices in this process to ensure that training sessions are on topics of value and interest to them?

5. Are training sessions hands-on and practice based? How do you currently encourage your teachers to take what they've learned in training and attempt to apply it in the classroom? Are there any follow-up routines or protocols in place to reinforce training sessions and ensure teachers feel supported during implementation?

6. Do teachers have access to coaching now? If so, how successful has that been? If not, what challenges might exist with introducing coaching as a long-term strategy for supporting teachers as they shift to blended learning?

7. Are you currently using PLCs? If so, how much time do your PLCs have together in a given day, week, or month? Is there any structure given to their time together? If you do not currently use PLCs, what might be the value of incorporating them into your schedule? What might the challenges of introducing PLCs be given your current schedule and school culture?

CHAPTER 3

School Community Leaders & Coaches

Blended Learning Requires Effective Professional Development

If, as a system, we really believed personalized learning and blended learning increase achievement, teachers might be asking why don't we structure their learning in the same way? What we do speaks louder than what we say.

—Sharon Wright (@shwright_co),
blended learning coach

INTRODUCTION

It's alarming how much professional development still employs a traditional "sit and get" lecture model. Even many conferences that advocate for innovative student-centered approaches to teaching with technology still follow a 50-minute session model in which teachers have no time to get their hands on the learning before the session is over and they are herded into the next room. Ironically, this one-size-fits-all training model is *exactly* what schools transitioning to blended learning are trying to move away from. Not only does this style of professional development not model what it advocates, but research shows that this approach is ineffective.

Despite these shortcomings, there are benefits to bringing in an expert to light a fire and get teachers excited about change. Because the shift from traditional teaching to blended learning is such a significant change, many teachers need to understand and experience the benefits in order to get on board with a shift that requires time, energy, and effort.

If a district brings in a blended learning expert to energize, inspire, and garner buy-in, the best approach is to use blended learning models and strategies to transform the traditional "sit and get" professional development session into a hands-on, practice-based, immersive experience that is more relevant and individualized. When done well, these trainings become the spark that can ignite change.

This chapter will:

- Identify the necessary elements of effective professional development

- Share a simple yet effective approach for training a group of teachers

- Encourage leaders to attend and actively participate in group trainings

- Highlight strategies to help coaches keep the learning going after the expert leaves

TRADITIONAL PROFESSIONAL DEVELOPMENT IS LARGELY INEFFECTIVE

Typically, teachers are paid to attend a handful of professional development days each school year wherein the entire staff is brought together in a common space to receive training. I use the word *receive* intentionally because teachers often play a passive role in these trainings. So it's not surprising that many teachers leave a training session feeling like the training did not speak to their specific needs or teaching assignment.

Unfortunately, traditional whole-staff professional development is still the norm for many districts despite the well-documented failings of this approach to create change in teacher practice. The Center for American Progress report titled *High-Quality Professional Development for Teachers* (DeMonte, 2013) identified the shortcomings of traditional professional development:

- It is usually disconnected from the everyday practice of teaching.

- It is too generic and unrelated to the curriculum or to the specific instructional problems teachers face.

- It is infrequent and implemented as a one-shot event or led by an outside consultant who drops in to conduct a workshop and never returns to the school or district. (DeMonte, 2013)

Teachers want training that feels relevant and immediately applicable. I often tell teachers during training that my goal is for them to leave with something they can use with their students the next day. I understand that every teacher faces specific challenges, so the goal for me as the trainer is to ensure that the training is built around the teachers, providing them with ample opportunities to take the ideas and strategies I am presenting and apply them to their own work.

Despite the challenges presented by traditional professional development, a skilled trainer with expertise in blended learning can help to establish the *why* behind this shift and articulate the value of moving from a traditional teacher-led approach to a student-centered approach with blended learning. The key is for the trainer to model this student-centered approach by using blended learning models in the training to place teachers at the center of learning. When the training places the focus on the teachers, not the trainer, then teachers have time to explore, discuss, collaborate, and create.

It's important that trainers understand where the school district and teachers currently are in the journey to blended learning. They must also be dynamic if they are to successfully provide the spark necessary to excite teachers about the changes taking place. Teachers, like students, need to know why they are being asked to make a big change that will require time, energy, and effort. They need to feel confident that this shift will benefit the learning outcomes for students as well as positively impact their teaching reality. If they believe blended learning will allow them to focus on the aspects of teaching they enjoy most—curriculum design and interactions with students—they will be more likely to embrace blended learning.

ELEMENTS OF EFFECTIVE PROFESSIONAL DEVELOPMENT

Regardless of the topic, the most effective professional development

- is ongoing,
- is specific to a teacher's subject area and grade level,
- employs the strategies it advocates that teachers use, and
- is practice based.

These elements of effective professional development are especially important when we talk about professional development aimed at supporting teachers who are shifting to blended learning. Not only does blended learning require a new approach to lesson design and execution, the teacher and student roles in the classroom shift, and technology is crucial to customizing instruction and personalizing practice for individual students. That's a tall order, especially for teachers with little to no technology training. All of these pieces require dynamic professional development opportunities coupled with one-on-one coaching and ongoing support as a member of a PLC.

Research conducted by Borko, Jacobs, and Koellner (2010) supports the need to rethink traditional professional development to include content that is "situated in practice," focuses on student learning, models instructional practices, places teachers in an active role as learners, and leverages PLCs where educators are encouraged to share knowledge in collaborative learning environments. Additionally, professional development opportunities and models must be ongoing and sustained. The challenge facing school districts is how to offer whole group training sessions that incorporate the elements of effective professional development and then build on that momentum with coaching and PLCs to ensure the excitement generated in an engaging large group training session drives real change.

Professional Development Should Be Ongoing

The duration of professional development is directly tied to its success. This makes intuitive sense. We know that the longer we spend learning about and practicing a specific skill, such as writing or playing the piano, the better we get. However, a report titled *Reviewing the Evidence on How Teacher Professional Development Affects Student Achievement* (Yoon, Duncan, Lee, Scarloss, & Shapely, 2007) pointed out that most schools and districts lack a coherent infrastructure for professional development, so "professional development represents a 'patchwork of opportunities—formal and informal, mandatory and voluntary, serendipitous and planned.'" This patchwork approach to planning learning opportunities for teachers leads to a series of disconnected learning experiences with little to no follow-up. Teachers, like students, need repeated exposure to ideas, time to practice, support, and feedback as they attempt to apply what they learn. This demands a more thoughtful and long-term vision when it comes to professional learning because the more time teachers spend engaged in professional learning, the more likely they are to make changes in their teaching practice. Corcoran, McVay, and Riordan (2003) analyzed research and concluded that "teachers showed the greatest change in practice after three years of participation and more than 80 hours of professional development. Prior to that tipping point, most teachers made only incremental changes in their practice" (p. 38).

Teachers, like students, need repeated exposure to ideas, time to practice, support, and feedback as they attempt to apply what they learn.

An expert who introduces blended learning can help teachers understand the theory behind the changes they are making, but teachers need ongoing support as they attempt to take the new strategies and apply them in their classrooms. Studies conducted by Joyce and Showers (2002) revealed that "teacher mastery of a new skill takes, on average, 20 separate instances of practice." It's the "instances of practice" part that's important to note. If we are going to make significant changes in education without alienating teachers, it's crucial to move beyond single-day staff trainings to embrace a long-term coaching model complemented by PLCs.

Professional development focused on blended learning needs to be ongoing because teachers need repeated exposure to and practice with the models and strategies. They also need targeted training using technology such as online technology tools, collaborative online work suites, learning management systems, adaptive software, and digital curriculum. Technology is changing rapidly, which means training must be consistent and ongoing. Teachers must have time to continually improve their teaching practice with a specific focus on using technology and blended learning models effectively.

> Technology is changing rapidly, which means training must be consistent and ongoing. Teachers must have time to continually improve their teaching practice with a specific focus on using technology and blended learning models effectively.

Professional Development Should Be Specific to a Teacher's Subject Area and Grade Level

Professional development should be customized for a teacher's grade level and subject area. Too often teachers leave a training session feeling like the information was not relevant to their specific teaching assignment. So not only is most training not effective because it is limited to a handful of days, but it is also not effective because it doesn't speak directly to the teacher's specific issues, challenges, and content standards.

For example, a third-grade teacher looking for strategies to teach research skills to her or his students will have different needs than a tenth-grade teacher who is also teaching research skills. A third-grade teacher might benefit from learning how to create a custom search engine to allow students the ability to hone search skills while limiting the scope of that research to sites that the teacher has identified as high quality, credible, and appropriate. Elementary teachers at a G Suite for Education school may want to learn how their students can share what they've learned by designing a multimedia poster using Google Drawing or a multimedia slide show using Google Slides.

By contrast, secondary teachers might prefer to learn how to support their students in evaluating the credibility of online web pages and designing infographics so the students can share their research. If these teachers attend the same workshop aimed at developing research skills, they are unlikely to get exactly what they need from that experience. This is why professional development that targets a specific grade level and/or subject area is most effective for introducing new strategies, technology tools, and blended learning models.

Blended learning adds another layer of complexity because teaching with technology requires not only technology skills but also a clear sense of which blended learning models will work in a given classroom. For example, an elementary classroom with eight iPads will want to begin with the Station Rotation model, in which students rotate through a series of online and offline stations. This would allow them to maximize their limited technology. By contrast, a high school class with 1:1 Chromebooks might prefer to begin with the Whole Group Rotation (previously called Lab Rotation), in which the entire class moves between online and offline work.

Professional Development Should Employ the Strategies It Advocates

Professional development is more effective when it uses the same strategies in training that it aims to have teachers adopt and use with their classrooms. If a facilitator is working with a group of teachers on the Flipped Classroom model, it would be beneficial to "flip" the instruction or explanation prior to the training to allow teachers to experience the model. Then when teachers come to the face-to-face training, that time can be spent discussing information and applying it in collaborative groups.

Now, you may be thinking, "Well, what if the teachers don't watch the video? That would throw a serious wrench into professional development." That's a valid concern, but it's the same exact scenario teachers are worried about when they envision trying the Flipped Classroom model with their students. Teachers always ask, "What if kids don't do their homework?" So why not address this with the group of teachers so they can see how a facilitator handles participants who come to "class" without engaging with the flipped content. The trainer can move those who watched the flipped video to a collaborative group activity where they work in content teams to construct a flipped lesson. Then the teachers who still need to watch the video start the training doing that before moving on to apply what they learned by planning their own flipped lesson. The group that has already watched the video will enjoy more time during the collaborative group activity.

The benefits of using the Flipped Classroom model in the training session are threefold: (1) All teachers—even those who didn't complete the flipped assignment prior to the training—experience a flipped lesson, (2) teachers are shown a strategy for managing individuals who do not complete the flipped assignment, and (3) teachers spend time working at their own pace with colleagues and dive deeper into concepts instead of simply listening to a trainer talk.

When I train teachers on blended learning models, I often use the Station Rotation model as a vehicle to introduce teachers to technology tools, lesson design, and facilitation strategies. Figure 3.1 depicts a training session focused on online discussions using the Station Rotation model. I designed this Station Rotation lesson to help teachers develop the skills and resources to facilitate successful online discussions while simultaneously introducing them to the Station Rotation model.

FIGURE 3.1 Using the Station Rotation Model in Teacher Trainings

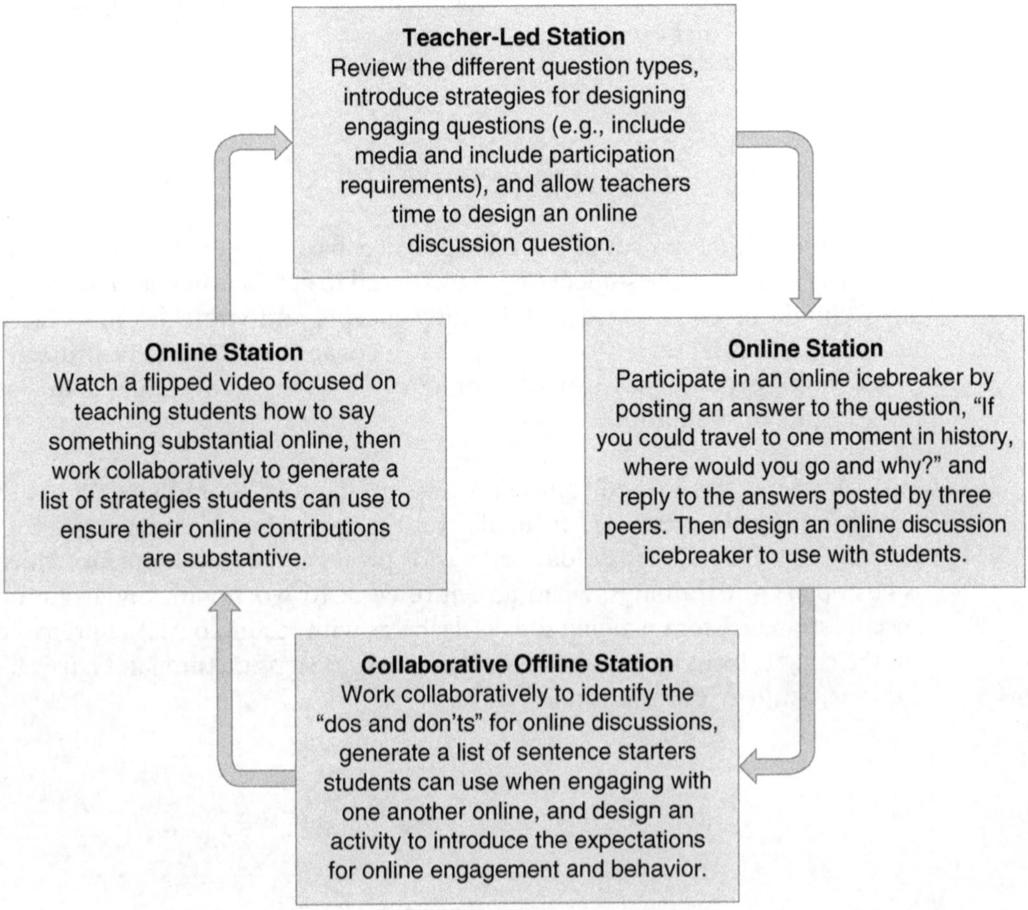

Teacher-Led Station
Review the different question types, introduce strategies for designing engaging questions (e.g., include media and include participation requirements), and allow teachers time to design an online discussion question.

Online Station
Watch a flipped video focused on teaching students how to say something substantial online, then work collaboratively to generate a list of strategies students can use to ensure their online contributions are substantive.

Online Station
Participate in an online icebreaker by posting an answer to the question, "If you could travel to one moment in history, where would you go and why?" and reply to the answers posted by three peers. Then design an online discussion icebreaker to use with students.

Collaborative Offline Station
Work collaboratively to identify the "dos and don'ts" for online discussions, generate a list of sentence starters students can use when engaging with one another online, and design an activity to introduce the expectations for online engagement and behavior.

The Station Rotation model makes it possible for me to work with smaller groups of teachers in my teacher-led station, showing them how to design quality online discussion questions. It also models the design of a station rotation by engaging them in a mix of online and offline tasks. Finally, it allows me to break teachers up into smaller learning communities so they are more likely to lean in and engage with each other and with the strategies I am introducing.

When an expert uses the models to engage teachers during the training session, this allows teachers to experience the models in the role of a student. This is extremely valuable. A teacher who has watched flipped content, moved through a station rotation, or followed a playlist to learn during a training session will have a much better sense of that model when they leave the session. All professional development should strive to employ the strategies it advocates. The days of "sit and get" learning—both in the classroom and in professional development—are over.

All professional development should strive to employ the strategies it advocates. The days of "sit and get" learning—both in the classroom and in professional development—are over.

Professional Development Should Be Practice Based

Professional development should be practice based to engage teachers in active learning. Just like students, educators need to get their hands on learning. They should be encouraged to take the concepts and strategies introduced and plan an actual lesson or activity that incorporates these new strategies or technology tools. They can also "practice" with their colleagues acting as the students in simulations.

Last summer I was invited to teach a class at Stanford's Graduate School of Education. Teachers traveled from all over the world for this intense week of learning. Instead of a single day or two of professional development, which is customary for trainings, I had an entire week to work with my group on specific strategies for engaging today's learners with technology. As I prepared for the course, I was encouraged to follow the four steps pictured in Figure 3.2 for every strategy I introduced.

FIGURE 3.2   A Simple Approach to Professional Learning

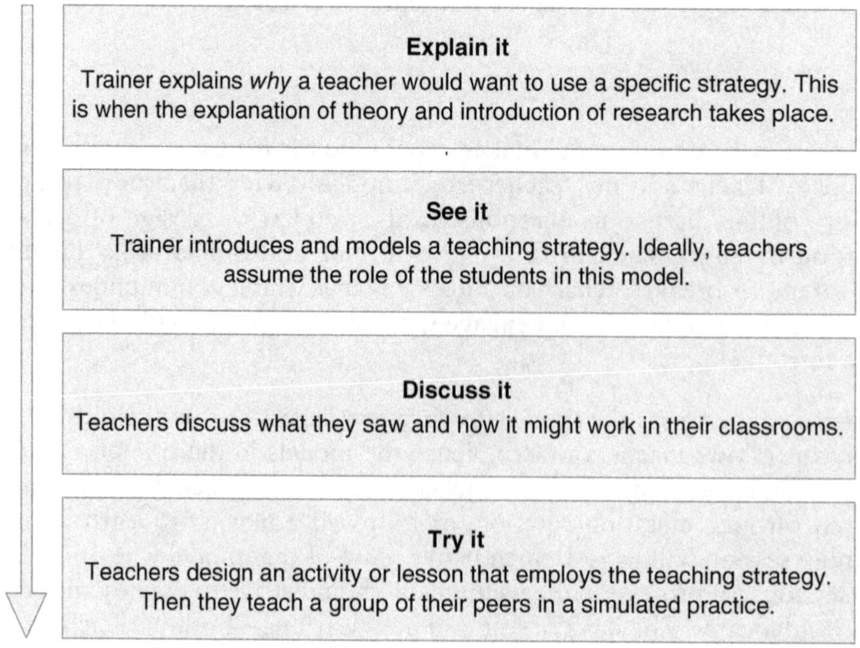

Explain it
Trainer explains *why* a teacher would want to use a specific strategy. This is when the explanation of theory and introduction of research takes place.

See it
Trainer introduces and models a teaching strategy. Ideally, teachers assume the role of the students in this model.

Discuss it
Teachers discuss what they saw and how it might work in their classrooms.

Try it
Teachers design an activity or lesson that employs the teaching strategy. Then they teach a group of their peers in a simulated practice.

This simple approach incorporates several key elements of effective professional development. According to research done by Joyce and Showers (2002), the four factors that are key to effective professional learning are (1) presentation of theory, (2) demonstration or modeling, (3) practice in a simulated setting, and (4) peer coaching.

In their research, Joyce and Showers specifically looked at the impact each of these factors had on classroom application. Even though some factors, such as the presentation of theory and modeling, have a low impact on student learning and others, such as coaching, have a very high impact, the key is that each of these factors must be part of a comprehensive approach to long-term professional development (Boyd, 2008).

If a trainer uses the four-step approach described below when working with a group of teachers, the trainer can create a firm foundation for change that coaches can build on. In fact, it's imperative that coaches participate in these training sessions to understand the theory and practice using the strategies, technology tools, and blended learning models alongside the teachers they coach.

Explain It

Just like students, teachers need to understand the *why*. *Why* are they being asked to change their approach? *What* are the benefits for them and their students? It's important that teachers understand the theory behind and objectives of a new approach, strategy, or model. This explanation should not dominate the bulk of professional development, but it should be presented to provide teachers a clear justification for why this is a worthwhile investment of their time and energy. Some districts choose to present the *why* in the form of a book study where members of the staff read a common text that answers the *why* in detail. This frees the trainer up to jump right into the "see it" phase of professional development described below.

During the "explain it" stage, teachers should be asking themselves:

- How does this strategy impact learning outcomes for students?
- Does this strategy give students more control over the time, place, pace, or path of their learning?
- How does this change my role in the learning? How does it change the student's role?
- How can I articulate this *why* to my own students?

See It

Teachers need to *see* the strategy in action. It's ideal if the person facilitating professional development treats the teachers as learners and places them in the role of the student during this phase of learning. When educators experience a strategy as the student, they are likely to have more questions and to appreciate the impact and benefits of the teaching strategy from the learner's perspective. Too often teachers try a strategy with students that they themselves have never experienced, so they lack empathy for the students when they struggle or have questions.

As teachers experience the strategy, they should consider the following questions:

- What is the teacher's role? What is he or she doing?

- What are we, the students, doing? What skills are we using or developing?

- What role is technology playing in this strategy or activity?

- What aspects of learning do we have control over in this moment?

- What is challenging and/or enjoyable about this activity?

Discuss It

Once teachers have seen—or better yet, experienced—a strategy, they need time to discuss what they saw with their peers. Unpacking a teaching strategy via discussion helps teachers to better understand the parts of the demonstration or model. The purpose of this conversation should be to ask questions about the aspects of the strategy or model they did not understand, explore the value of the strategy, and brainstorm what implementing the strategy might look like in their classrooms. This will prepare teachers for the next step, which will ask them to apply the strategy in a simulated classroom.

As they discuss the strategy or model, teachers should consider the following questions:

- How is this strategy different from my current approach?

- How would this strategy work in my classroom? When would I use this strategy?

- What preparation would need to take place to execute this strategy?

- What questions and/or concerns do I have about using this strategy?

- How could this strategy improve learning outcomes for my students?

Try It

Implementation is the hardest part of trying something new. The moment when a teacher attempts to implement a new strategy is the moment she or he will most likely hit a bump and become frustrated or disillusioned. Without a robust support network, one failure to successfully implement a new strategy can result in a teacher abandoning the strategy because the implementation did not look like the model or demonstration he or she experienced in training. That is why it's so important for teachers to have an opportunity to practice a strategy in the actual training with peers.

Not only does trying a strategy out with colleagues provide teachers with a safe space to test their ideas and receive feedback on their initial attempts at implementation, it also creates a level of accountability. If teachers know they will be asked to take what they have seen and design a sample activity or lesson that implements a specific teaching strategy and use that to teach a group of their peers, the level of buy-in is much higher in professional development. They will pay attention because they are being asked to take an active role in applying the new concepts, strategies, and/or models.

> If teachers know they will be asked to take what they have seen and design a sample activity or lesson that implements a specific teaching strategy and use that to teach a group of their peers, the level of buy-in is much higher in professional development.

As teachers try out a teaching strategy with each other, it's important that the teachers who are in the role of learners in the simulation consider the following questions:

- Are the objectives of the activity clear?
- Are the steps clear? Do I know what I am supposed to do?
- Would any additional information, media, time, etc. have helped me to be more successful during this activity?
- Did the role of technology, if used, improve or impede the learning?
- How was this simulation similar to or different from the model?

This is an excellent approach for practice-based professional development with a group. However, this is just the first step. Coaching is the long-term strategy that builds on professional development to ensure that teachers are supported as they take what they have learned and apply it in their own classrooms. The University of Florida Lastinger Center for Learning, Learning Forward, and Public Impact report titled *Coaching for Impact* (2016) stated,

> Teachers typically need close to 50 hours of learning and practice in an area to improve their skills and their students' learning. Researchers have described the "implementation dip" of practice—the awkward and frustrating period that occurs when teachers integrate a new skill into existing practice. During this time, they need support to push through to mastery.

The coach is an essential support system and sounding board in the process of taking what the teachers learn and applying it to their classrooms to, in turn, improve student learning.

Obviously, an expert that comes into a school district to train teachers will not provide the ongoing support teachers need during implementation. Given the time constraints of the training, the expert may not be able to make the training specific to every teacher and subject area. However, experts can and should employ the strategies they advocate for and use a hands-on, practice-based approach to professional learning.

Using the various models in combination with the "explain it, see it, discuss it, try it" method will also make the training feel more personalized. Teachers need the opportunity to talk about a new strategy or model, think about what it might look like in their classroom, and practice designing lessons that they can use with their own students. This is possible in a large group training session, but it's imperative that the expert structure the training to allow teachers the time and space to get this done. That means an expert will cover less ground in a training session, but what is sacrificed in terms of breadth will be made up by the depth of learning happening.

LEADERS MUST LEAN IN

Leaders must be willing to lean into the learning. If an expert is hired to facilitate a training session, leadership members should be actively engaged in learning right alongside their teachers. Unfortunately, the majority of the trainings I facilitate are devoid of leadership. There might be an instructional coach or professional development coordinator in attendance, but rarely does anyone in a leadership position attend. This is a missed opportunity. Every member of a school community must be engaged in professional learning.

> If an expert is hired to facilitate a training session, leadership members should be actively engaged in learning right alongside their teachers.

One of the biggest challenges a leader faces when trying to make a large-scale change such as a shift to blended learning is teacher buy-in. Teachers often feel like decisions are made in a top-down manner. Leadership decides to move the school in a particular direction, then teachers are asked to make significant changes that require time—a luxury most teachers don't have in abundance. This disconnect between leadership and teachers can be bridged in large part if leaders attend training sessions to better understand the challenges, concerns, and needs of their teachers.

During training, I frequently field questions or work with teachers to troubleshoot challenges they may face as they take the blended learning models back to their classrooms. Leaders are best equipped to make decisions that will positively impact teachers and support implementation, but if they don't attend the training they cannot anticipate the challenges their staff may face. For example, if a teacher is really excited about the Station Rotation model but worries that the bulky furniture in her classroom will make moving around the space challenging, that's something leadership should hear. There might be opportunities to switch furniture with another room or order some smaller, more movable pieces of furniture for classrooms.

> Leaders are best equipped to make decisions that will positively impact teachers and support implementation, but if they don't attend the training they cannot anticipate the challenges their staff may face.

When leadership makes the time to attend training sessions, it also sends a clear message that the entire school community is committed to learning. This translates into leaders with a better understanding of the shifts they are asking teachers to make and teachers who are more willing to take risks because they feel supported. If leaders and teachers learn side by side, it creates an honest dialogue about learning that's invaluable as a school embarks on a big change.

Leaders who do attend training should actively engage with their teachers and the content. I've led a few workshops where school leaders or administrators attend but spend the entire time at a back table responding to e-mails. If teachers see leaders disengaged at a training session or focused on other work, it sends the message that the training is not worth their time and attention. This is counterproductive and can cause teachers to question why they are being asked to attend a session that those in leadership aren't willing to invest their own energy and effort into.

WRAP UP

In the past schools have relied on a handful of professional development days each year to help their teachers continue learning and refining their practice. An expert or trainer is hired and teachers spend the day learning. However, this traditional model isn't effective on its own. Teachers report feeling like these sessions aren't relevant to their specific teaching assignments and are too infrequent to support them through the challenges of implementation. Teachers need repeated exposure to teaching strategies, blended learning models, and technology tools.

Instead of being the end of the learning, these training sessions with an expert should serve as the spark. If an expert engages the group in hands-on, practice-based training using the "explain it, see it, discuss it, and try it" approach, he or she is more likely to excite teachers and garner buy-in. Then the coaches and professional learning community will create the learning infrastructure needed to support teachers as they take what they learned and implement those strategies and models in their classrooms. This is why it's crucial for leaders, coaches, and teachers to attend these training sessions together.

BOOK STUDY QUESTIONS

1. How often does your school bring in an expert to train teachers? How successful have these sessions been? How do you evaluate the success of a group training session led by an expert?

2. When you bring in an expert to work with teachers, is there a strategy for following up on that learning? Is there an expectation that teachers will implement what they learned? If so, how does leadership track implementation after a training session?

3. What format do your group training sessions typically take? Are experts encouraged to make training hands-on or follow an "explain it, see it, discuss it, try it" format? Who communicates with experts hired prior to training? How can you ensure that experts follow a hands-on, practice-based approach to working with teachers?

4. Do blended learning training sessions currently employ the strategies they advocate for? If not, what opportunities do you see to use blended learning models to improve professional learning on your campus?

5. Do leaders attend training? How might participation by leadership impact the move to blended learning? What impact might their engagement and involvement have on the overall success of a blended learning initiative?

CHAPTER 4

School Community Leaders & Coaches

The Blended Learning Coach

If we could personalize professional learning like we do for our students at school, we'd be on the right track.

—Ashley Pacholewski (@BHSPacholewski),
ELA teacher and instructional coach

INTRODUCTION

Embracing blended learning is a huge shift for traditional teachers. On the surface, blended learning requires a new approach to lesson design and facilitation; on a deeper level, it requires a completely different mindset. Ultimately, teachers must accept that they no longer need to be a fountain of knowledge and that their energy is better spent as an architect of learning experiences, a coach providing real-time support and feedback, and an analyzer of data to shape individual learning paths.

The professional learning infrastructure on a campus must support this shift in mindset to help teachers to (1) understand the value of their new role, (2) learn how to place students at the center of learning in the classroom, and (3) select the blended learning model or models that best meet their learning objectives and work well with the resources available. A coach with experience teaching in a blended setting is likely to be the most authentic and effective support system for teachers making this shift.

A blended learning coach can guide teachers through this transition, providing them with the necessary training, support, and feedback needed to navigate these new waters. The blended learning coach can build on the

43

excitement and interest created during the spark, or whole group training, to ensure that teachers feel confident designing blended lessons, utilizing technology effectively, and implementing lessons that weave together active, engaged learning online and offline.

This chapter will:

- Define the role of a blended learning coach
- Identify the five elements of effective coaching
- Explore both the teacher role and student role in a blended classroom
- Provide an overview of the blended learning models
- Highlight the coach's role in this changing educational landscape
- Identify the benefits of coaching as a part-time position for strong teachers

COACHING IN A BLENDED LEARNING CONTEXT

The job of a blended learning coach is to support teachers as they shift from traditional teaching strategies to using blended learning models to engage students in active learning online and offline. Ideally, the blended learning coach has three specific areas of expertise: experienced educator, technology enthusiast, and trained coach, as pictured in Figure 4.1.

FIGURE 4.1 The Blended Learning Coach

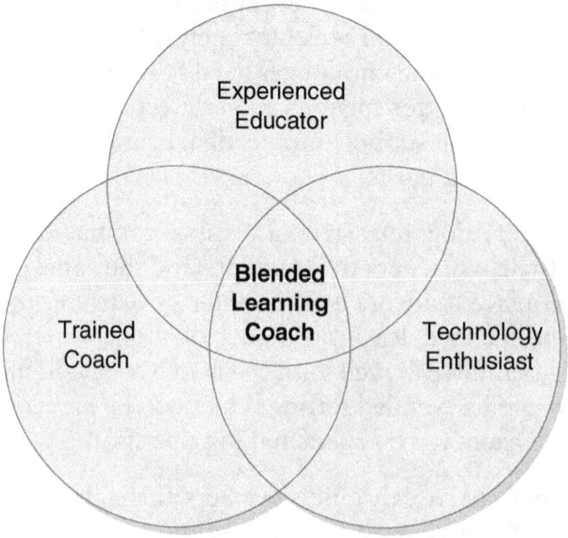

It's important for a blended learning coach to have classroom experience because a strong pedagogical foundation combined with experience designing and facilitating blended lessons and managing a classroom creates credibility. Classroom experience makes a coach more realistic, more empathetic, and better equipped to support a teacher transitioning from a traditional teaching model to a blended learning model. If the teacher being coached doesn't feel confident that the coach has a clear understanding and appreciation of how complex teaching is, then the relationship is less likely to be productive.

Blended learning is grounded in the belief that combining face-to-face learning with online learning has the potential to improve learning outcomes for students. The technology component is critical to blended learning, so it's helpful for the blended learning coach to be a technology enthusiast. Different teachers will have different needs, so a strong working knowledge of the technology tools and online resources available can help the coach to support a wide range of teachers. This doesn't mean the coach has to be an expert on all aspects of technology, but she or he should be excited about technology and have a strong understanding of the various blended learning models. Because technology changes so quickly, a blended learning coach who enjoys playing with technology and exploring new tools will be the best resource for teachers.

Finally, an effective coach also needs the right disposition for coaching and some training on coaching. There are some experienced teachers who love technology but who would not make a strong candidate for a blended learning coach because of their personality or demeanor. The coaching relationship must be built on a foundation of respect and trust. This means the blended learning coach must treat the teachers they work with as equals, listen actively, and communicate effectively. Some coaching strategies can be learned, as evidenced in this book, and other qualities are innate. The delicate balance of qualities needed to be a successful blended learning coach makes the job of identifying and recruiting these people challenging. Once leadership has found coaches to support the shift to blended learning, it's crucial that the coaches understand what effective coaching entails.

ELEMENTS OF EFFECTIVE COACHING

My favorite definition of coaching comes from a meta-analysis of research on coaching conducted by Kraft, Blazar, and Hogan (2017). In their paper, they characterized

> the coaching process as one where instructional experts work with teachers to discuss classroom practice in a way that is (a) individualized—coaching sessions are one-on-one; (b) intensive—coaches and teachers interact at least every couple of weeks; (c) sustained—teachers receive coaching over an extended period of time; (d) context-specific—teachers are coached on their practices within the context of their own classroom; and (e) focused—coaches work with teachers to engage in deliberate practice of specific skills. (p. 9)

The description of coaching as individualized, intensive, sustained, context-specific, and focused makes so much sense in the context of blended learning coaching, as described in Figure 4.2.

Blended learning is evolving quickly because technology, online resources, adaptive software, and digital curriculum are rapidly changing and improving. This necessitates a new approach to training teachers, especially those who are already in the field and who never received targeted training on how to use technology to engage learners.

FIGURE 4.2   Elements of Effective Coaching for Blended Learning

Individualized	Just like our students, teachers are in wildly different places when it comes to their skill sets. Some are early adopters excited to try new teaching techniques, while others are more reluctant to experiment. Some teachers are comfortable with technology and learn how to use new tools quickly and enjoy exploring online tools, but others do not. This makes an individualized approach to coaching in a blended learning context more effective. Just as blended learning seeks to personalize learning for individual students, blended learning coaching should aim to do the same for teachers.
Intensive	Unlike traditional forms of professional development that tend to span a single day or at best a series of days, the best coaching is intensive and ongoing. There are several different aspects of transitioning to blended learning, from lesson planning to implementation. It's ideal if the blended learning coach can complete the coaching cycle detailed in this book to support the teacher through the complete process of planning, executing, and reflecting on their blended lessons.
Sustained	Different teachers will require different amounts of time and coaching, so this too should be individualized based on need. The research on how much time is needed for coaching to be effective is unclear, but some teachers will need sustained and ongoing support as they attempt to transition from traditional teaching techniques to blended instruction.
Context-specific	Every classroom and teaching assignment is different. Coaching provides support that is specific to the teacher's exact circumstance. Some teachers are lucky enough to teach in a 1:1 setting with a device for every student, while others only have a handful of devices in their classrooms. Some schools have invested heavily in digital curriculum, learning management systems, and adaptive software, while others encourage teachers to use free technology tools that work best for their specific discipline. Each circumstance will lend itself to particular blended learning models. If blended learning coaching is context specific, it will be more useful and sustainable.
Focused	*Blended learning* and *technology* are huge umbrella terms, so the best blended learning coaching will focus on one model, one strategy, or one technology tool at a time. The more focused the coaching, the more manageable it will feel. Too often teachers feel pressure to do it all or learn it all at once, which isn't realistic when we are talking about shifting teaching practices to weave together online and offline work. The best strategy is to start small and then expand.

The blended learning coach must teach, model, and provide feedback. Ideally, a blended learning coach is a master teacher with a solid understanding of the various models and an expert at using technology for learning. Since technology tools, online resources, learning management systems, online productivity suites, and digital curriculum are constantly changing and being updated, it's crucial that blended learning coaches receive specialized training in these areas to best support the teachers they are working with.

BLENDED LEARNING COACHES CONTINUE THE LEARNING

Learning is a process. Teachers know that a single day of training is unlikely to have an impact on their teaching practice. To create real change, professional learning must be intensive and sustained. Teachers need support from beginning to end. Unfortunately, many districts invest in the spark and bring in an expert who only serves to introduce a new strategy or approach to teaching. Then the teacher is left to wrestle with the details and attempt to implement without any support. As noted in Chapter 2, it is during this implementation when most teachers are likely to get frustrated and disillusioned and, ultimately, to abandon a new approach. This is why the bulk of this book (Chapters 5–11) is focused on the role of the blended learning coach in professional learning. It is the coach who will keep the learning going long after the expert has left the building.

The blended learning coach must take the spark created in the whole group training or all-staff professional development day and keep it alive with individualized, intensive, context-specific, and focused professional learning. These key elements to successful coaching can be accomplished as coaches move through the blended learning coaching cycle with individual teachers. It is during this cycle that the coach can help individual teachers take the ideas and general strategies introduced in the whole group training and apply them to his or her specific teaching assignment.

The positive impacts of coaching cannot be understated. Joyce and Showers (2003) found that compared to uncoached teachers, coached teachers "practiced new strategies more often and with greater skill," "adapted the strategies more appropriately to their own goals," "retained and increased skill over time," and "were more likely to explain the new models of teaching to their students" (p. 3). Ultimately, coaches help teachers to take new ideas, strategies, models, and methodologies from training and implement them more consistently and successfully than teachers who don't have a coach. If the blended learning coach moves through the coaching cycle pictured in Figure 4.3 (on the next page), she or he can support teachers from start to finish. The coach can take the excitement generated by the spark to ensure teachers successfully implement blended learning models to improve learning outcomes for students.

FIGURE 4.3 Blended Learning Coaching Cycle

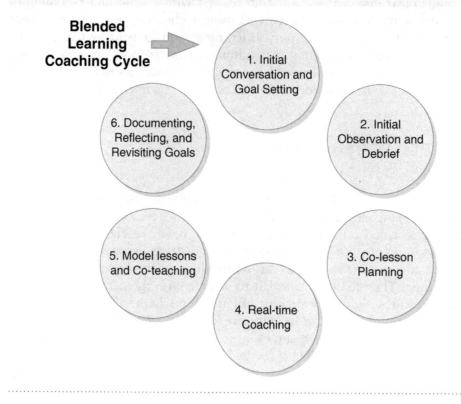

REDEFINING TEACHER AND STUDENT ROLES IN A BLENDED LEARNING ENVIRONMENT

The teacher's role in the classroom fundamentally changes when he or she moves from whole group lessons to blended lessons. The teacher becomes an architect of learning experiences, weaving together face-to-face and online learning to provide students with more control over the time, place, pace, and path of their learning. The teacher also becomes a coach focused on supporting the development of specific skills.

In a blended learning environment, the teacher becomes an architect of learning experiences, weaving together face-to-face and online learning to provide students with more control over the time, place, pace, and path of their learning.

Instead of standing at the front of the room, a teacher in a blended classroom is working with individual students or small groups of students to support the development of specific skills, as illustrated in Figure 4.4. Because the focus in a blended classroom is on the student, not the teacher, students must take a more active and engaged role in learning; they can no longer be passive

FIGURE 4.4 Shifting Roles in a Blended Learning Environment

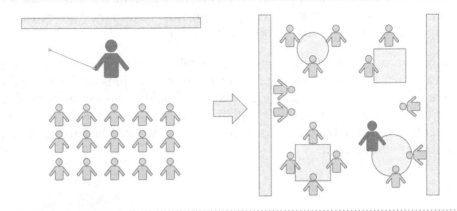

participants in school. I find it comical to watch students with call slips enter my classroom because they always stop at the door, look slightly confused, and scan the room to find "the teacher." Because I rarely stand at the front of the room and more commonly sit next to a student or group of students, I am hard to identify. These moments remind me how different my role is in the classroom compared to when I first began teaching 16 years ago.

The best examples of blended classrooms feel more like learning hubs. Students sit in pairs, small groups, or individually working on a range of tasks depending on their individual needs as a learner. The teacher is on hand to answer questions, lend support, and provide necessary follow-up instruction, modeling, and scaffolds. In turn, the learner knows how to access information, troubleshoot with peers, and use technology effectively to learn. This creates a learning environment that is more flexible and personalized.

A QUICK REVIEW OF BLENDED LEARNING MODELS

Blended learning is constantly changing and evolving. It's important to think of this newer space in education as malleable. Too often in training or coaching sessions teachers ask me, "Is this right?" I remind them that there isn't one "right" way to execute blended learning. Some teachers select a single model and use that consistently with students; other teachers mix and match using several different models with their students. I've always been a fan of what I describe as the "teacher-designed blend," where the individual teacher uses whichever model or models best serve a lesson or learning objective. I frequently mix the Station Rotation, Flipped Classroom, Whole Group Rotation, and Individual Rotation/Playlist models in my own classroom.

The best blended learning coaches are the ones who are flexible. They've had experience with different models and support teachers in finding the best fit for their class, subject area, age group, and learning objectives. Instead of forcing a one-size-fits-all approach to blended learning on a teacher, they use observations and conversations to figure out what makes the most sense for the specific teacher they are working with.

Below is an overview of the established models currently in use; however, it is important to note that there are many different variations on these models. These definitions are just a starting place and should by no means be used to limit teachers transitioning to blended learning. Definitions are only valuable in that they give us a language to talk about ideas; they can be harmful if they are seen as an endpoint.

The Rotation Models

The Rotation model and its submodels are designed for students who are learning primarily on a brick-and-mortar campus. The Christensen Institute (2018) defined the Rotation model as "a course or subject in which students rotate on a fixed schedule or at the teacher's discretion between learning modalities, at least one of which is online learning. Other modalities might include activities such as small-group or full-class instruction, group projects, individual tutoring, and pencil-and-paper assignments." This definition allows for a myriad of variations, including Station Rotation, Whole Group (previously referred to as Lab Rotation), Flipped Classroom, and Individual Rotation/Playlist.

Each of the subcategories of the Rotation model described in Figure 4.5 allows students to rotate through online and offline learning activities. The teachers play a key role in designing the learning and deciding what blend

FIGURE 4.5 Common Variations of the Rotation Model

Station Rotation	Students are learning primarily in a school setting and rotate through learning stations, with at least one station dedicated to online learning. In this model, the teacher has time to work with small groups of students at a teacher-led station.
Whole Group Rotation or Lab Rotation	The entire class rotates through a series of online and offline activities together while remaining in a single classroom or moving between a classroom and a computer lab. When the class is working online, the teacher is freed up to work with individual students.
Flipped Classroom	The transfer of information is moved online so students can self-pace, and the practice and application is moved into the classroom so students have the benefit of the subject area expert and a community of peers to help support them as they apply new information.
Individual Rotation/Playlist	Students move through online and face-to-face learning on a highly personalized path. They have an individual playlist created by the teacher or an algorithm that dictates what learning activities a single student will move through.

of online and face-to-face work will be most beneficial for students and/or most plausible given their access to technology both in and outside of school.

Flex Model

The Flex model relies heavily on online learning, which becomes the backbone of the course. Students have a teacher on-site who provides varying degrees of individual face-to-face support while students "move on an individually customized, fluid schedule among learning modalities" (Horn & Staker, 2014, p. 56). The Flex model is designed to provide teachers and students with more flexibility because "online learning does much of the heavy lifting in terms of delivering instruction" (Maxwell, 2016). This requires a robust online curriculum, but it frees the teachers from standing at the front of the room lecturing or delivering content. The teacher can move into a coaching role, customizing support for individual students as they progress through the learning activities.

A La Carte Model

The A La Carte model is an online course that is added to a student's menu of courses. A student may be enrolled at a school that does not offer a particular class, so he or she can opt to take that class online to supplement the school's offerings. Similarly, a student who failed a class or is missing credits can take a class a la carte from a third party online to make up those lost or missing credits while still enrolled at a brick-and-mortar school. Unlike the Flex model, the teacher of record for the A La Carte model is online, so the learning can take place either at school or off-site.

Enriched Virtual Model

The Enriched Virtual model, like the Flex and A La Carte models, is grounded in online learning; however, the students have "required face-to-face learning sessions with their teacher of record and then are free to complete their remaining coursework remote from the face-to-face teacher" (Horn & Staker, 2014, p. 57). These meetings do not occur daily but are an important aspect of the course. Blending this online learning with face-to-face time with the teacher provides students with a more comprehensive school experience. The online teacher and face-to-face teacher in the Enriched Virtual model are usually the same person.

The various blended learning models reflect a spectrum, as pictured in Figure 4.6, with some models being more conducive for a traditional school shifting to blended learning (e.g., Rotation) and others perhaps working best at a school designed to support blended learning (e.g., Enriched Virtual). Each district and school will need to identify which models make the most sense given its school structure, facilities, personnel, student body, and technology infrastructure and hardware.

FIGURE 4.6 The Spectrum of Blended Learning Models

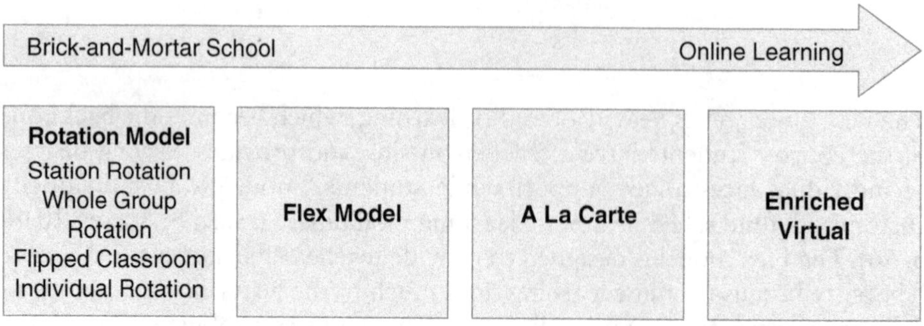

Brick-and-Mortar School	Online Learning →

Rotation Model Station Rotation Whole Group Rotation Flipped Classroom Individual Rotation	**Flex Model**	**A La Carte**	**Enriched Virtual**

BLENDED LEARNING: ESTABLISH A CLEAR PLAN

Some schools begin with a single model and focus on supporting teachers as they learn how to use that particular model in their classrooms; the goal is to expand to other models once teachers have a firm understanding of the first model. Other schools prefer to introduce teachers to a few of the models at the same time and allow the teachers to decide which models make the most sense for their curriculum and learning objectives.

When I began working with elementary teachers in Healdsburg the goal was to get teachers using and comfortable with the Station Rotation model because they wanted to maximize limited technology and create time for small group instruction. By contrast, I worked with a high school district outside of Phoenix, Arizona, that purchased Edgenuity. They wanted to use a Flex model in which the online learning available via Edgenuity was central to the learning and teachers were focused on individualizing support. These two different districts selected models they felt would be the best fit for their teachers, students, and technology access.

For a school district just getting started on its blended learning journey, I'd recommend my last book, *Blended Learning in Action* (Tucker et al., 2016), which provides a guide for schools shifting to blended learning. It speaks to the big decisions leaders must make regarding device, learning management, and digital curriculum purchases and provides a roadmap for change. It also has teacher-facing chapters that provide in-depth explanations about the various models and resources for lesson planning and troubleshooting common hurdles, which can be valuable to teachers and coaches.

CHALLENGES FACING THE CREATION OF A COACHING CULTURE

In my experience working with coaches in a district, I see three fairly consistent challenges associated with coaching assignments:

1. Coaches are typically talented, tech-savvy educators who have been plucked from the classroom to coach full time, thus distancing them from students and shared teacher experiences.

2. Coaches tend to have a large teacher-to-coach ratio, making it challenging to support individual teachers.

3. Coaches don't have dedicated time with the teachers.

So, let's explore these common challenges facing coaches and, subsequently, a school community striving toward innovative change by adopting a coaching culture.

Challenge #1: Taking Teachers out of Classrooms

When a school decides to employ coaching as a strategy to train teachers, administration often looks to its own talented, technology-savvy teachers first. Those individuals are often plucked from the classroom and tasked with the job of coaching their peers. It makes logical sense to take your most tech-talented teachers and let them share their knowledge.

I both understand and lament the decision to take these teachers out of the classroom completely and put them in a new role supporting their colleagues. I realize that administration needs these teachers to lead the charge and help their more reluctant peers to experiment and take risks. At the same time, I hate to see incredible teachers leave the classroom entirely. I can't help but think about all of the students who won't benefit from that teacher's passion and expertise.

There is also an age divide when it comes to technology and who is using it. Generally, younger teachers who have grown up with technology are more comfortable experimenting with it in the classroom. Established veteran teachers who entered the profession without any technology training are then left to be coached by younger and less experienced teachers. It is easy to see how this divide can create resentment and frustration. It immediately creates a disconnect between the coach and the coachee.

When I'm hired to lead professional development at a school site, I often communicate directly with the coaches prior to the event. They provide insight about where their teachers are in the shift to blended learning and help me to identify specific content that would be most relevant or helpful for their teachers. During these conversations and later when I am on-site actually leading professional development, I often feel a real "us versus them" tension between the coaches and teachers. The coaches want to help but often feel frustrated by their teachers' unwillingness to try new teaching techniques and technology. Simultaneously, the teachers resent being asked to do even more when they already feel swamped.

This is one reason I believe it's most effective if a blended learning coach teaches half of the time and coaches half of the time. This balance translates into coaches who have more credibility with the teachers they coach because they are still in the classroom facing the same daily challenges the teachers they work with face. They also have a classroom to try out new ideas, so they can continue to share authentic examples with the teachers they are coaching. In fact, their classrooms can be "open" spaces where the teachers they work with can come and observe the coach using the models and technology. Seeing blended learning models and technology in action is a powerful strategy for getting reluctant teachers on board with change.

> It's most effective if a blended learning coach teaches half of the time and coaches half of the time.

As a teacher and a coach myself, my work in the classroom makes me a better coach, and my coaching makes me a more thoughtful teacher. When I am coaching teachers who are shifting from a traditional teaching model to a blended learning model, I am able to draw on my experiences and failures to emphasize that this is a journey. It makes me more relatable and coaching less scary. Conversely, I am often inspired by my work with other creative teachers and am able to take ideas that blossom from our coaching sessions and use them in my own classroom.

Challenge #2: Coach-to-Teacher Ratio

Just as a large class size can make reaching and supporting individual students more challenging, coaches face the same challenge when their coach-to-teacher ratio is too high. I've worked in districts where a single coach is responsible for supporting 100+ teachers. This makes using a systematic coaching cycle with each teacher impossible. There just aren't enough hours in the day or weeks in the year. A school district committed to transitioning to blended learning must keep the coach-to-teacher ratio realistic for one-on-one coaching to be possible.

If financial constraints limit the total number of coaches at a school site, then it's important for the school leader to decide how to pair coaches and teachers to maximize coaching. For example, I worked with a group of teachers in Longmont, Colorado, who are part of a blended collaborative designed to give them special training throughout the year so they can become strong practitioners of blended learning. In this case, the district is investing time and energy into training a relatively small group of excited early adopters who can then lead the transition to blended learning. In other districts I've seen the coaching begin with a single subject area, like math. This pilot approach to training a small group of teachers as opposed to a whole staff is one way to keep the coach-to-teacher ratio lower.

Challenge #3: Dedicated Time

Coaching demands time, but time is a luxury most teachers don't have. If coaching is going to be successful, leadership at a school must make sure that there is a clear understanding about how much time a coach and teacher will be working together. Coaching time must be prioritized during a teacher's preparation period and may require release time for the teacher and coach to meet. Too often when coaching is not prioritized and time is not set aside for the coach and teacher to work together, coaches end up spending the bulk of their time attempting to share information virtually. Although there are merits to scaling coaching with virtual sessions, as will be discussed in Chapter 11, virtual coaching is different from populating a Twitter feed with links or creating a YouTube playlist of video tutorials.

Ultimately, if coaches do not get one-on-one face time with the teachers they work with, they will begin to feel disillusioned and ineffective in their positions. It's important for both the coach and teacher to have dedicated time together.

WRAP UP

Ideally, the blended learning coach is an experienced educator with a firm understanding of the various blended learning models and a willingness to learn about and experiment with new technology tools and online resources. The blended learning coach should have expertise in teaching and technology as well as the temperament required to work well with others.

As blended learning coaches work with teachers, the goal is to offer support that is individualized, intensive, sustained, context specific, and focused. These five elements have been identified as crucial to the overall success of a coaching program. The coach will need to tailor coaching to the individual teachers to ensure that it meets their specific needs. The coach will also need to make key decisions about how much coaching is needed since every teacher will progress through the coaching cycle at a different rate.

Coaches tend to experience similar challenges in their roles supporting teachers. They tend to face resistance from the teachers they work with, they have large coach-to-teacher ratios that make one-on-one coaching impossible, and they don't have dedicated time set aside to work with teachers. These challenges can make it hard for them to support the teachers they are working with. It's crucial that leadership members consider how they can help coaches to avoid these common issues by employing coaches that still teach part time, using a pilot approach to keeping the coach-to-teacher ratio manageable, and allocating time to the coaching process.

BOOK STUDY QUESTIONS

1. What makes a blended learning coach similar to or different from other types of coaches (e.g., literacy coach or content-specific coach)? What additional skills or training might the blended learning coach need to be successful?

2. How can a blended learning coach support the transition from large group training to individual implementation? What strategy should the blended learning coach use when selecting the first round of teachers to work with? Who are the best candidates for this first round of coaching?

3. Review Figure 4.2: Elements of Effective Coaching for Blended Learning and discuss these elements of effective coaching. How are these elements evident in your current approach to professional learning? Which elements are missing?

4. How does shifting from a traditional teaching model to blended learning models impact both the teacher and student roles in the classroom? What challenges might these shifting roles create? How can a blended learning coach help to support a teacher in this transition?

5. Given your school's structure, facilities, personnel, student body, and technology infrastructure and hardware, which blended learning model or models might work best? Will you introduce a single model at a time or several all at once? Will teachers have the opportunity to select the model or models that work best for them or will this decision be made by leadership?

6. Given the common challenges facing coaches that were identified in this chapter, how can leaders support coaches to ensure they are able to work one-on-one with teachers to help them transition to blended learning? How can some of these common challenges facing coaches be avoided or mitigated?

CHAPTER 5

BL
Coach

Coaching: Initial Conversation and Goal Setting

I utilize a backwards design approach when working with teachers. We identify the end goal, break it into action steps, then set a timeline from beginning of process to the end goal. I've found breaking a large task into small chunks reduces stress and promotes forward progress with fidelity.

—Karen McKinley (@TheELALady), edtech trainer, ELA consultant, and gifted coordinator

INTRODUCTION

In his book, *Unmistakable Impact*, Jim Knight (2011a) explored the role of authentic dialogue in professional learning. Knight described dialogue as "talking with the goal of digging deeper and exploring ideas together" (p. 38). From this perspective, dialogue is a "way of communicating where there is equity between speakers, where ideas are shared, and where every partner's ideas are respected" (Knight, 2011a, p. 38). When working with teachers transitioning to blended learning, coaches must strive for conversations grounded in equity and respect. The coach must be a partner.

Dialogic interviews are a unique format designed to create a space for honest dialogue aimed at helping each person to better understand the other's experiences, values, and motivations. Once that foundation has been laid, the coach can guide the teacher in articulating SMART goals that are specific, measurable, attainable, relevant, and timely. This chapter provides a resource with helpful questions to guide and document the goal-setting process.

This chapter will:

- Introduce the dialogic interview format
- Provide a dialogic interview guide to use in your initial conversations
- Outline the process and purpose of setting SMART goals

THE POWER OF DIALOGIC INTERVIEWS

I attended a Deeper Learning Conference in San Diego, and one of the most powerful experiences I had occurred on the first day. Directly after the keynote address, attendees were sent to individual classrooms for a "dialogic interview." This was a totally unfamiliar concept to me, and I wasn't sure what to expect when I took my seat in the classroom at High-Tech High.

Our facilitator explained that participants would pair up and have 30 minutes to participate in this conversation. She told us that for the first 15 minutes, one person would ask the questions and listen while the other person would be the respondent answering the questions. Then we should switch roles for the final 15 minutes.

I found a partner and settled in for our dialogic interview. The facilitator gave us one final word of warning: "Resist the urge to interject your own stories and reactions when you are the questioner." Unlike a typical conversation where there is a natural back and forth, this was an exercise in being a dedicated and active listener and then transitioning into the role of honest and open responder.

I began as the questioner. As I listened to my partner, a librarian from Virginia, answer questions such as, "What was your life like growing up?" and, "Why did you become an educator?" I was drawn into her story, and with every question she elaborated a little more and shared interesting details about her life and how various events had shaped her. I found I really enjoyed listening to her story. There were so many points of commonality between her life experiences and my own that it was hard at times not to jump in and share my own anecdotes, but I appreciated that allowing her to speak uninterrupted for the whole 15 minutes created more continuity and encouraged her to share details she might not have if we were bouncing the questions back and forth. At the end of our interview, I felt like I had made a new friend. I now had an intimate connection with this person I had only met 30 minutes before. It surprised me how quickly you can come to know another person in the right situation. I knew I wanted to use this format with the teachers I coach.

On the opposite page is a resource that coaches can print out or access digitally and use in their initial conversations with the teachers they are coaching. It explains why the coach is using this format, outlines the process, and provides interview questions for the coach to use during the dialogic interview.

DIALOGIC INTERVIEW

Blended learning coaching requires that the coach and teacher work closely together over an extended period of time. This relationship necessitates that both parties know and trust one another. The shift to blended learning often requires teachers to take risks in their classrooms, which is less scary if they feel understood and supported by their coach. This initial conversation is designed to create a foundation of respect and understanding between the coach and the teacher. This foundation is essential to the long-term success of this partnership.

THE PROCESS:

Review the process together prior to your conversation.

- This conversation will take 30 minutes.
- For the first 15 minutes, the questioner will ask questions and the responder will respond, then you'll switch roles. Instead of taking turns answering each question, this format allows for more continuity and encourages a deeper level of response.
- The questioner should set an alarm on his/her phone to keep track of the time.
- When you are the questioner, your job is to listen attentively and resist the urge to interject your own reactions or stories. However you are welcome to ask follow-up or clarifying questions. For example, you might ask, "Tell me more about . . ." or, "How did that impact you?"
- The coach should *not* take notes during this conversation. There is a 5-minute written reflection that follows this conversation where you'll have the opportunity to capture your thoughts and reflections.
- Depending on the conversation, you may or may not get through all of the questions below. You may also find you are inspired to ask additional questions that are not on this list.

INTERVIEW QUESTIONS:

You are *not* limited to these questions, but they are a good place to start. It's okay if you do not get through them all.

1. What were your schooling experiences like growing up?
2. Why did you become an educator? Why are you an educator now?
3. Tell me about your teaching assignment. Describe your class or classes.
4. How successful do you feel you are at adjusting for students at different levels?
5. What is most rewarding about your position? What is most challenging?
6. What do you feel is the value of using technology in education? What fears do you have about teaching with technology?
7. What would your perfect classroom look like? Describe it.
8. What do you wish you had more time for?
9. What does teacher success *look* like for you?
10. What does student success *look* like?

POST INTERVIEW REFLECTION PROMPT:

Write a brief reflection on your experience participating in the dialogic interview.

- What insights did you gain during this conversation?
- What questions do you have that were not answered?
- Did this conversation help you to identify any goals you have for yourself as an educator?

 Available for download at bit.ly/DialogicInterview.

It's important for the teacher to feel *heard*, so the coach needs to actively listen, make eye contact, and avoid interrupting during the dialogic interview. As the responder, it's also helpful if the coach is really honest about his or her experiences as an educator. It will help the teacher feel more comfortable being open and honest if the coach models this in the interview. In fact, if the teacher does not have a preference, then it might be best for the coach to be the responder first in the dialogic interview to set the tone for the conversation.

After the dialogic interview, the coach and teacher should both take 5 minutes to consider the experience and any takeaways from it in a written reflection. This is when the coach can capture any specifics about the teacher's teaching assignment, note specific insights gained, and/or list additional questions that surfaced as a result of the dialogic interview. These notes will be especially helpful to the coach if he or she is working with multiple teachers at one time. Once the dialogic interview and written reflection are complete, the coach should guide the teacher through the process of setting goals. The coach and teacher will revisit, revise, and update these goals throughout the coaching cycle.

SMART GOAL SETTING

When setting goals it's crucial to engage teachers in the process so they feel invested in achieving those goals. Thus, the goals must stem from a teacher's values and what she or he believes will improve learning. Jim Knight (2011a) made the point that "people are motivated by doing work that makes a difference" (p. 27), so teachers should focus their goals on improving aspects of their teaching that will have a real impact on student learning. The teacher may need guidance identifying realistic goals with outcomes that are attainable and can be measured. The more concrete the goal-setting process, the more likely it is to be successful.

In 1981 George T. Doran wrote a paper titled "There's a S.M.A.R.T. Way to Write Management's Goals and Objectives." Doran (1981) introduced the mnemonic acronym SMART, which has in the years since been co-opted by countless organizations. It is a simple strategy for developing goals that are realistic and achievable. The SMART approach makes goal setting less daunting and abstract for both teachers and coaches. As a coach, it's easier to sit with a teacher and talk about setting goals if you have a clear method to guide that conversation and produce something tangible that can be revisited.

According to the SMART acronym, goals should be:

- Specific
- Measurable
- Attainable
- Relevant
- Timely

Goals Should Be Specific

Articulating specific goals is more challenging than making general sweeping statements about change, so it's the coach's job to ensure that teachers are keeping the focus of their goals narrow so they do not become overwhelmed as they attempt to achieve their goals. For example, instead of saying, "I want to use more technology in my classroom," teachers should identify a more specific goal, such as, "I want to design and implement my first Station Rotation lesson by September 15th" or, "I'd like to set up my YouTube channel by the end of next week."

It's better to have several small-scale, specific goals than one or two broad goals. As teachers achieve their specific goals, they will gain confidence and feel more capable of tackling more challenging goals. It's also important to emphasize that a specific goal will be easier to both attain and measure.

Here are some questions to guide your goal-setting conversation:

- What would you like to specifically accomplish in terms of using technology in your classroom this week, month, and semester?

- Which piece of technology would you like to build into a lesson next week?

- Is there a particular blended learning model (e.g., Station Rotation) or technology tool (e.g., Google Classroom) you want to begin using with students?

- When, where, and how will you achieve each goal?

Goals Should Be Measurable

There are a variety of ways to measure whether a goal has been successfully reached. You will need to determine the criteria for evaluating if a goal has been accomplished with your teacher. If the teacher's goal is to design and implement a Station Rotation lesson by September 15th, he or she might be able to measure the success of that goal by simply looking at the calendar to see if a Station Rotation lesson was actually designed and facilitated by that date; however, it's worth encouraging the teacher to think about what "success" looks like on a deeper level. Perhaps she or he can design a student survey using a Google Form or an Exit Ticket to collect student feedback on the lesson to see what students enjoyed or what tips they have for improving the lesson in the future.

Teachers may also want to evaluate engagement levels, the number of students who complete an assignment, or the scores on an assessment. Encourage your teachers to decide how they plan to measure the success of a particular goal. If it cannot be easily measured, that may be a sign that the goal is not specific enough.

Here are some questions to guide your conversation about measuring goal success:

- What would success look like for this particular goal?

- How much would implementing this blended learning model impact student engagement, assignment completion rates, and/or test scores on the next assessment?

- How will you know when you've successfully accomplished this goal? What will you be looking for specifically as markers of success?

- Can you engage your students in evaluating the success of this goal?

Goals Should Be Attainable

It's easy for a teacher working with technology to become overwhelmed. Technology is changing rapidly, and new technology tools pop up all the time. If teachers feel they have to "master" technology or rethink everything they are doing to fit it into a blended learning model, you'll likely find them overwhelmed and resistant to try anything new. Instead, goals must be realistic and attainable. It must be something the teacher is willing, able, and excited to work toward. That's why it's best if the teacher articulates a goal he or she is excited to pursue and not one that is mandated by the school or administrative team.

Here are some questions to guide your conversation about goal attainment:

- Is your goal within reach given your access to resources and/or time, and are there competing priorities that affect this goal? If any of these considerations will negatively affect your goal, can you adjust your goal to make it more realistic?

- What specific support or materials will you need to accomplish this goal?

- Are there any factors that may make this goal hard to realize? How can those factors be mitigated?

Teachers are keenly aware of all the obstacles that could make it challenging to try something new or achieve a goal, so this is where an optimistic trouble-shooting coach is invaluable. If a teacher is concerned about having enough devices for a station, then the coach should help the teacher to identify a strategy for securing technology. If a teacher is worried about having time to plan a Station Rotation lesson, let him or her know you'll be meeting to help and can focus on designing the lesson together.

Goals Should Be Relevant

Making sure a goal is relevant for the teacher is absolutely crucial to buy-in and follow-through. If the goal is only relevant because it is a mandate from administration, it's unlikely to motivate your teacher. Instead, focus this part of the goal-setting conversation on how this goal will improve the learning experience for students and how it can allow the teacher to focus on the aspects of the job that he or she enjoys most.

If a teacher says, "I need to design and implement a Station Rotation lesson because my principal expects me to use this model," encourage the teacher to identify the value of the actual model. Highlight that a Station Rotation lesson will allow the teacher to create smaller learning communities within the larger class and provide an opportunity for her or him to work individually with students to customize instruction and personalize feedback. It's the coach's job to highlight the benefits of the various blended learning models and/or technology tools that teachers are being asked to use.

If the teacher really struggles to articulate the value of using a particular blended learning model or technology tool, it would be a good idea to facilitate an observation of another class where the model or tool is being used effectively or set up a time for the coach to design and facilitate a model lesson, as described in Chapter 9. Sometimes seeing a model or tool in action can help a teacher better appreciate its value.

Here are some questions to guide your conversation about goal relevance:

- Why do you *want* to reach this goal?
- How does this goal complement your school's culture or the culture in your specific classroom?
- How will it improve learning outcomes for students?
- How will it improve your experience as a teacher?

Goals Should Be Timely

Teachers already feel they are in a race against time, so it's the coach's job to make sure any deadlines set in pursuit of a goal are realistic. Attaching a timeline to each goal will prioritize that goal and create a sense of urgency. As most teachers can attest, the school day flies by. Without due dates or hard deadlines, it's easy to put off trying something new.

It's beneficial for a coach to have a shared Google Calendar with his or her teachers to keep track of important dates. This way there is a level of transparency about when each goal should be accomplished. A Google Calendar is easy to adjust in case a timeline ends up being unrealistic because there are state tests happening that cut into class time or a field trip is planned last minute. Stuff happens, so a coach needs to be flexible.

Here are some questions to guide your conversation about the timeliness of goals:

- When will you accomplish this goal? Do you have a specific date you can put in the calendar?

- Will you need to follow a specific timeline to ensure you succeed in accomplishing this goal? If so, how do you plan to break up the steps needed to accomplish this goal?

- Is there a checklist you can create with individual due dates to keep you on track?

On the opposite page is a resource you can print out or share digitally with your teachers to walk them through the SMART method of goal setting. This will make it easy to revisit goals as you work with your individual teachers. In fact, I'd recommend that coaches create a folder for each of their teachers in their Google Drive or on their computers so it's easy to organize their individual documents and track their progress.

FIGURE 5.1 SMART Goal Setting

What are your goals?

Once you've articulated your goal[s], reflect on how it's specific, measurable, attainable, relevant, and timely.

SPECIFIC	MEASURABLE	ATTAINABLE	RELEVANT	TIMELY
What would you like to specifically accomplish in terms of using technology in your classroom this month? When, where, and how will you achieve each specific goal?	What would success look like for this particular goal? Can you engage your students in evaluating the success of this goal? How will you know when you've successfully accomplished this goal?	Is your goal within reach given your access to resources and/or time, and are there competing priorities that affect this goal? If any of these considerations will negatively affect your goal, can you adjust your goal to make it more realistic? What specific support or materials will you need to accomplish this goal?	Why do you *want* to reach this goal? How does this goal complement your school's culture or the culture in your classroom? How does it improve learning outcomes for students?	When will you accomplish this goal? Do you have a specific date you can put in the calendar? Will you follow a specific timeline or break up the steps? Is there a checklist you can create with individual due dates?

online
resources ⚓ Available for download at bit.ly/BLsmartgoals.

WRAP UP

It's normal for a teacher to feel threatened by the prospect of making major changes in his or her teaching practice. Working with a coach may initially cause feelings of unease, so the first conversation needs to establish commonality between the coach and the teacher. This initial conversation is an opportunity to make a connection and set a tone for the work a coach and a teacher do together. Dialogic interviews encourage each party in the conversation to listen attentively and respond honestly. This can lead to an appreciation of how each individual has been shaped by her or his past experiences and how that might impact the individual's perceptions of teaching and learning.

Once a foundation has been established in a dialogic interview, the coach and teacher must identify clear goals that are specific, measurable, attainable, relevant, and timely. This should be a collaborative exercise, with the coach guiding the conversation to ensure goals fit the SMART criteria. As the teacher articulates his or her goals, those goals should be entered into a shared document that can be revisited throughout your work together. Goal setting makes the shift to blended learning more concrete for teachers by encouraging them to start small and focus on one change at a time. It also provides a roadmap for their work with their coach.

BOOK STUDY QUESTIONS

1. What are your initial thoughts on the dialogic interview format? How might this yield different results compared to a traditional conversation?

2. Are there any questions you would add to the dialogic interview resource provided in this chapter?

3. Why is goal setting so important to the long-term success of a blended learning shift? Do you think using the SMART approach to goal setting will help you guide teachers in setting realistic goals?

4. How often do you plan to revisit the goals set by your teachers? How can you and your teachers keep track of their goals together (e.g., shared Google Calendar or organizational app)?

CHAPTER 6

BL
Coach

Coaching: Initial Observation and Debrief

Teachers need ongoing support. It isn't simply about teaching them about a new process or tool. Without the ongoing support of a trusted and knowledgeable colleague, teachers will almost always fall back to what is safe, habit, or routine. When it comes to inspiring innovation and encouraging educational change for the 21st century, teachers need to know someone has their back and will be there to work with them through the inevitable challenges that come.

—Jenni LaBrie (@jennilabrie), instructional technology coach and Spanish teacher

INTRODUCTION

Being observed can be a nerve-wracking experience. For teachers embarking on blended learning, the initial observation is the moment in the coaching cycle when they feel most vulnerable. They have not yet received one-on-one coaching and may not feel confident implementing blended learning models. It's easy for a teacher to feel that an observation opens the door for judgment, so the coach must communicate to the teacher that their work together is a partnership.

The coach should clearly communicate the purpose of the observation and emphasize that it is non-evaluative and designed to get a feel for the way the teacher is currently designing and facilitating lessons. If a coach is using an observation guide or rubric, like The New Teacher Project (TNTP) Core Teaching Rubric, she or he should share the observation guide or rubric with the teacher in advance. In addition, notes generated during an observation should be shared directly with the teacher to help him or her better understand what the coach saw during the observation. The more transparency a coach creates during this stage of the coaching cycle, the more valuable the experience will be for teachers and the more likely teachers will appreciate, instead of fear, the process.

This chapter will:

- Articulate a clear goal for observations
- Provide a guide for your initial observation
- Encourage coaches to explain their role to students
- Provide questions the coach can use in the follow-up/debrief conversation

COACHING MUST BE A PARTNERSHIP

In Jim Knight's (2011b) article, "What Good Coaches Do," he identified seven partnership principles that are key to a respectful and productive coaching relationship. He said the way coaches view their role can have a huge impact on their success. He encouraged coaches to "take a partnership approach to collaboration" and stated that "partnership principles of equality, choice, voice, reflection, dialogue, praxis, and reciprocity provide a conceptual language that coaches can use to describe how they strive to work with teachers." These principles are particularly important to establishing the necessary trust and respect needed for a coach to engage in real-time coaching. Figure 6.1 identifies and defines each partnership principle, as presented by Knight (2011b), and describes what that looks like in the context of coaching.

FIGURE 6.1 Jim Knight's Partnership Principles in Practice

PARTNERSHIP PRINCIPLE	DEFINITION AND IMPACT	IN PRACTICE
Equality	Coach views and treats the teacher as an equal. Teachers are less likely to resist the shift to blended learning if they feel like they have an equal partner in the learning process. Teachers don't want to be told what to do, but most teachers thrive in collaborative situations with colleagues.	• Listens and observes attentively • Asks questions and makes suggestions instead of giving directions • Makes time for collaboration, brainstorming, and problem-solving • Keeps focus on teacher's goals • Strives to support teacher in his/her practice
Choice	Coach respects that the teacher will make the final decision about a teaching strategy or lesson. Teachers are more open to experimentation and change if they enjoy agency and are able to make key decisions in the process.	• Identifies different options or approaches and encourages the teacher to make decisions • Serves as a sounding board as the teacher decides which strategies, models, or tools to use or how to adjust a lesson in progress • Respects the teacher's decisions • Encourages teacher to consider SMART goals when making decisions

PARTNERSHIP PRINCIPLE	DEFINITION AND IMPACT	IN PRACTICE
Voice	Coach engages in and encourages honest conversations. Teachers feel more comfortable taking risks if they can share their excitement, concerns, and questions.	• Asks thoughtful questions about how the teacher is feeling • Creates time and space for candid conversations • Uses documentation from lessons to drive follow-up conversations and reflections on what worked and what needs improvement
Reflection	Coach builds in time to reflect and revisit SMART goals. Teachers can appreciate their own growth if they reflect on what they are doing and how it is impacting learning outcomes for students.	• Encourages teachers to watch and reflect on video footage of a lesson or documentation collected • Helps make connections between the reflection and SMART goals
Dialogue	Coach engages in dialogue with teachers to troubleshoot challenges, generate ideas, and refine strategies. Teachers need to talk through challenges and brainstorm solutions. Engaging in conversations with the coach provides the teacher with a sounding board to continue improving and refining her/his approach.	• Asks questions to engage the teacher in conversations about a strategy or lesson • Listens and offers suggestions • Highlights what is working well
Praxis	Coach helps teacher to apply new knowledge and skills. Teachers need the most support during the implementation stage. The coach can help teachers to take what they learned about a blended learning model or technology tool in a group training session and figure out what that could look like in their classroom.	• Supports teachers in the design of lessons • Explains the benefits of using a particular model, strategy, or technology tool • Suggests modifications to improve the lesson • Highlights strategies and skills the teacher is applying successfully • Reminds teachers of strategies that might be useful during a lesson
Reciprocity	Coaches treat every moment with the teacher as an opportunity to learn. Teachers have a wealth of knowledge and talents. The most successful coaching relationships are grounded in the belief that both teacher and coach have something to learn from their work together.	• Acknowledges great ideas • Builds on ideas shared • Thanks teachers for inspiring a new approach • Celebrates the co-creation that occurs in coaching sessions • Complements a new approach that works well

When a true partnership between teacher and coach is achieved, the teacher understands the purpose of feedback is to support and encourage. In fact, the best sign of a strong partnership is the teacher's willingness to engage in real-time coaching, as will be explored in Chapter 8, where aspects of the lesson are discussed openly and honestly with the goal of improving learning outcomes for students. This is achievable when the coach is committed to the partnership principles.

WHAT'S THE GOAL OF THE INITIAL OBSERVATION?

The goal of the initial observation is to get a feel for where a teacher is at in terms of his or her blended learning journey prior to coaching. Some teachers may be excited about using technology and experimenting with different blended learning models, while others may be hesitant.

As I conduct an initial observation, I think about the following:

- How is technology being used? What curricula, programs, technology tools, and/or online resources are currently in use?

- How is the room set up? Do students sit in small groups, pairs, or rows? Who is the focus—the teacher or the students?

- What is a typical lesson like? What are kids doing? How varied are the activities? How often do they rotate from one activity to another? How are transitions handled?

- How engaged are students in their learning? Do they seem interested in the activities and on task? How much autonomy do they enjoy?

- Do students have opportunities to control the pace of their learning?

- What is the teacher's primary role in the classroom? What is the student's primary role?

In addition to observing the way the teacher is currently designing and facilitating lessons, the coach gets a clear picture of the classroom and students. It's important to understand the composition of the class and the classroom norms, routines, management strategies, and physical layout. All of these factors impact a teacher's success and will ultimately influence what the coach and teacher focus on in their lesson-planning session. If a teacher needs support with classroom management, it's important to review strategies for establishing clear expectations for behavior and managing students effectively when they are using technology. If a teacher spends large amounts of time introducing information, then it may be helpful to talk about recording short videos or shifting the responsibility of reviewing information to small groups of students.

Prior to this initial interview it's important to be transparent with your teacher and let him or her know what you will be looking for and taking notes on during the observation. If the teacher understands that you want to capture a snapshot of his or her room, lesson, and students so you can use that to inform your work moving forward and not to cast judgment, then the initial observation will be less stressful for the teacher.

In addition, sharing the document you are going to use to capture your notes with the teacher ahead of time provides some insight into the aspects of her or his teaching that may become the focus of your work together. The initial observation guide that follows is a resource that a coach can use and/or modify to guide the first observation.

INITIAL OBSERVATION NOTES

	THINGS TO DO AND CONSIDER:	YOUR NOTES:
Physical layout	Draw a rough sketch of the room. • What type of furniture is in the room? • How is it arranged? Where is the focus? • Are there different types of learning spaces or zones?	
Composition of the class	• How many students are in this class? • What is the gender breakdown of students? • Are there students who clearly need additional support? • Are there students who seem disengaged or disruptive?	
Technology	• What hardware is available in the room? • Are there desktops or iPads, or is there a Chromebook cart? • How is the technology being used? Are students working individually or collaboratively using technology? • What types of online programs or digital curriculum is being used?	
Lesson	• What is the objective of the lesson? • How is the lesson broken up? Document time spent on each activity.	

(Continued)

(Continued)

THINGS TO DO AND CONSIDER:	YOUR NOTES:
• Who is the focus in each activity—teacher or student?	
• What is the content being covered?	
• What skills are students being asked to employ?	
• Do students work individually, in pairs, or in small groups?	
• Is the instruction, practice, or activity differentiated or personalized?	
• Is technology being used in any part of the lesson? If so, how?	

 Available for download at bit.ly/BLinitialobservation.

NOTES

Sharing the document on the previous page with the teacher being observed creates transparency about what was captured during the observation. However, it does require that coaches stay objective and focus on recording what they saw and not what they think about what they saw.

These observation notes can serve as a mirror, allowing the teacher to see the lesson from an objective perspective. As any teacher can attest, lessons can take unexpected detours. An explanation or modeling session scheduled for 5 minutes can easily take 15 if students are confused or ask a lot of questions. In the moment the teacher may not realize that she or he spent so much time on one activity or another. Similarly, it is hard to monitor the entire room, so a student might be off task searching for YouTube videos instead of completing the online practice activity. These are aspects of the lesson that the coach may be more equipped to notice during an observation.

COMMUNICATING WITH STUDENTS

Any time an adult other than the teacher enters a classroom, it is an event for students. All heads turn and they are immediately curious about the newcomer. Since the coach will be a repeated guest in the classroom, it's important that the coach take the time to introduce himself or herself to the students so they know who the coach is and why the coach is there. This will ultimately make them more comfortable with the coach's presence, which is important because the coach wants them to be relaxed and engage naturally with the content and one another.

When I began coaching teachers at Healdsburg Elementary School, I introduced myself in the classrooms. I explained that I have been a teacher for 16 years and was now also working with teachers as a coach to support them as they used technology. I asked the students, "How many of you have played a sport, like soccer or t-ball?" Several hands went up. I explained, "Just like a soccer or t-ball coach helps you learn the game and improve on your skills, that's similar to my work. My job is to support you and your teacher as you use technology to learn." The sports coach analogy is a pretty easy one for most students to grasp because they've played a sport or watched professional sports on television. I want students to know that I am there as a support system for them and their teacher.

In this first introduction I also highlight the importance of continuing to learn and grow no matter what you do in life. It's valuable for students to realize that anyone at any point in his or her life can benefit from coaching and continuing to develop and grow. It sends an important message about the value of lifelong learning. If teachers who have many years of experience are open to coaching, then students may not feel so bad making mistakes and asking for help.

> It's valuable for students to realize that anyone at any point in his or her life can benefit from coaching and continuing to develop and grow.

If we have time, I let students ask me questions they have about my role as a coach. They are curious little beings and I don't want to be a mystery. I want them to feel comfortable with me since I will be in their classroom co-teaching and providing real-time coaching feedback as I continue to work with their teacher.

THE DEBRIEF

The coach should schedule time directly following the initial observation to talk through the lesson with the teacher. If the coach shares the observation notes with the teacher, then those notes can serve as a helpful guide for this conversation. As a coach goes through the sections of the observation form, it will make it easier to talk about everything from the physical setup of the classroom to the design of the lesson.

It's important to allow the teacher the opportunity to add missing details or correct any misinformation in the observation notes. Students may have been absent or away from the classroom receiving additional support, and this would impact total numbers or the general composition of the class. There may have been elements of the lesson that were adjusted for skill level that the coach missed in the observation. Giving teachers an opportunity to fill the gaps in the observation notes can help them feel confident that the coach captured an accurate picture of the class. Once the coach and teacher have reviewed the observation notes, coaches should engage the teacher in a follow-up conversation about aspects of the lesson and lesson design that may not have been easily observed.

Hillsborough County Public Schools has developed pre- and post-observation guides designed to facilitate conversations about observations. Coaches looking to explore additional resources to aid in conducting effective observations and providing meaningful feedback may want to explore the TNTP Reimagine Teaching website (tntp.org). It has more than 450 resources curated from more than 50 schools and districts; these resources come in several formats, from ready to use, to some assembly required, to build your own.

Below are questions inspired by the Hillsborough County Public Schools pre- and post-observation resources, which can be found on the TNTP Reimagine Teaching website (tntp.org).

- Why did you choose this particular lesson objective[s]? Do you feel you successfully achieved this learning objective[s]? What data will you use to determine whether or not the learning objective[s] was met?

- Where are you in relation to this content—initial introduction or moving toward mastery?

- Did you use any student data to prepare for and design this lesson?

- Did you anticipate that students would struggle with any part of this lesson? If so, how did you prepare for that?

- How did you group students for this lesson? Did you differentiate or adjust for different skill levels? How do students who need additional support access it?

- Were there next steps or extension opportunities for students who were ready to move ahead or be challenged further?

- Which elements of this lesson will be assessed? What type of feedback will students receive? What is the timeline for that feedback? Do students play an active role in providing each other with feedback?

- Which aspects of the lesson went well? Which aspects of the lesson need to be modified or refined? Did you capture these reflective notes after a lesson to help guide future lessons? If not, how might you build a quick reflection (typed notes on a Google Doc or audio notes on your phone) into your routine?

- *How did you decide which blended learning model to use? What made this model attractive given the lesson objective[s]? Did you feel this blended learning model worked well? Why or why not?

- *How did you decide when and where to use technology? What did technology replace or improve, or how did it allow students to do something they otherwise could not have done? Did the technology work as expected?

*Questions for teachers already beginning to use blended learning models and technology

As with most of the other resources a coach uses, it is always a good practice to share a copy of the questions you plan to use with the teacher. I'd suggest pulling the most relevant questions and printing out two copies—one for you and one for your teacher—so you're not tempted to stare at a screen during the debrief conversation. Screens can be a distraction during face-to-face conversations, so I encourage coaches to keep the debrief offline. In fact, I don't typically take notes during this conversation because that can disrupt the flow, make teachers self-conscious, and be a distraction. Instead, I listen attentively, ask follow-up questions, and make sure to spend 15 minutes after our conversation jotting down the most salient points so I can remember them as we continue our work together.

REVISIT **SMART** GOALS

The best way to wrap up a conversation about a lesson is to revisit your teacher's SMART goals. Often individual goals are easy to lose sight of in the day-to-day work of lesson planning and teaching. You may have a teacher who says, "I wasn't even thinking about those when I designed this lesson." By pulling goal setting back into the conversation, the coach reminds the teacher that goals should drive decision making.

For example, if the teacher set a goal of using online resources to more effectively support students at different reading levels but did not use technology at all in the lesson, that's worth noting and discussing. This is where the coach can help the teacher to consider where adding technology could have helped make reading more accessible for students at different reading levels. Similarly, a teacher may set the goal of recording a video lesson to use in the first unit to allow students to self-pace through information. If the teacher did *not* end up using a video in the unit but the coach sees how the video could have been useful, then the coach can provide suggestions for how the unit could be modified to incorporate a video effectively.

Reviewing these goals and discussing how they impacted the teacher's decision making as he or she developed and facilitated the lesson is important. It keeps the goals established in the initial conversation at the forefront of the teacher's mind as he or she reflects on the current lesson and plans future lessons.

WRAP UP

Observations are critical to providing the coach with an accurate picture of the teacher's classroom, lesson design, and facilitation style. This window into the classroom will drive the lesson-planning session that follows. The better sense a coach has of where an individual teacher is in his or her blended learning journey, the more effective their work together will be.

As with all aspects of the coaching cycle, transparency is key. Teachers should know what to expect from an observation, students should know who a coach is and why she or he is in the classroom, and observation notes should be a shared resource. This transparency alleviates fear and anxiety for both teachers and students.

BOOK STUDY QUESTIONS

1. How might the partnership principles help coaches avoid resistance in their work with teachers? How could you as a coach employ the partnership principles in this early stage of coaching to put teachers at ease?

2. During an observation, what are you looking for specifically? Are there any aspects of a lesson you would want to make notes about that were not explicitly covered in the Initial Observation Notes resource provided in this chapter?

3. Would you share the Initial Observation Notes resource with your teacher prior to your observation or after? What would the benefits of sharing this document be? What might be challenging about sharing these notes? How would these notes be valuable in future steps of the coaching cycle?

4. How might you use these observations during the lesson-planning, co-teaching, real-time coaching, and documenting and reflecting steps in the coaching cycle?

5. Are there additional questions you would add to a question bank for the debrief conversations? If so, what might you want to discuss? Will you provide questions to the teacher ahead of time?

6. How would you use the SMART goals in the debrief? How can you tie the conversation about the lesson you observed to the goals you set in your previous session?

CHAPTER 7

Coaching: Co-lesson Planning

I think the most important thing teachers need help with is reflecting on why they are using a technology tool and how it fits in with best instructional practice. Most teachers can learn where to click and how to operate a tool, but if they don't consider how this technology can shape learning in their classroom, the use of the technology is empty.

—Kyle Dunbar (@edtechdunny),
technology integration specialist

INTRODUCTION

Lesson planning for a blended environment requires teachers weave together online and face-to-face elements. The more seamlessly these pieces fit together in a lesson, the more successful the lesson will be. Because many teachers leave their credential school without training in designing blended lessons, the job of educating teachers falls on school districts. Although a whole group training session can provide teachers with basic strategies and lesson templates, one-on-one coaching sessions can help teachers select the best model and technology tools for the specific goals of a given lesson.

As a blended learning coach, my favorite moments working with teachers occur during our co-lesson planning time. This stage in the coaching cycle is when most teachers realize that I am their ally. I'm there to support them *and* I can offer something valuable. I can help them plan lessons that weave together technology and tradition to improve learning outcomes for students. The key is to use these one-on-one coaching sessions to actually create lessons, not just talk about what the teacher needs to do when she or he leaves our coaching session. Teachers are busy, so these sessions must be hands-on and productive.

This chapter will:

- Highlight best practices for lesson-planning sessions between coaches and teachers
- Provide lesson templates
- Introduce a strategy for building reflection into the lesson-planning process

COMMUNICATE WITH THE TEACHER AHEAD OF TIME

Prior to the lesson-planning session, it's important to communicate directly with the teacher you are coaching to ensure she or he comes prepared with the necessary materials needed to create a blended lesson. I always e-mail teachers to request that they bring the following:

- Lesson planner
- SMART goals
- Device
  - Teacher device
  - Student device
- Curriculum and lesson-planning materials
- Standards for reference

Communicating prior to the lesson-planning meeting will ensure the teacher has all the tools he or she will need so you can make the most of your time together.

MEET OUTSIDE OF THE CLASSROOM

I have met with teachers both in their classrooms and in a neutral space, such as a small conference room, and I prefer the neutral space. It helps to eliminate distractions. When teachers work in their rooms during a prep period, they are surrounded by reminders of things they have to do—stacks of ungraded student work, notifications alerting them to parent e-mails, and cluttered desks. All of these distractions can make it hard for the teacher to focus on the lesson planning. Also, often our sessions are interrupted by other staff members stopping by the classroom to ask a question or say hello. This can make it challenging to get through the development and creation of an entire blended lesson. As a coach, I connect with administration to find out what spaces are available on campus for us to use, then I coordinate booking those spaces as needed. I prefer spaces where we have access to a big whiteboard where we can visually sketch out lesson concepts and overviews.

IDENTIFY THE GOALS

It's important to start any lesson-planning session by asking the teacher to fill you in on what he or she is covering right now. Some questions to ask include the following:

- Tell me about yesterday's lesson.
- What do you want to cover in the lesson we are designing today?
- What are the learning objectives?
- Which blended learning model do you want to use for this lesson?
- Do you have an idea of how you'd like to use technology in this lesson?
- Do you have any questions or concerns before we get started?

The coach must quickly establish that this planning session will be driven by the teacher, not the coach. If the teacher feels the coach is coming into a lesson-planning session with an agenda, the session is less likely to feel relevant to the challenges and curriculum the teacher is concerned about in that moment. The more relevant this lesson-planning session is, the more likely the teacher is to follow through in actually implementing the lesson.

KEEP THE LESSON MANAGEABLE:
THINK BIG, BUT START SMALL

The initial conversation may lead to both short-term goals and long-term goals. However, it's important to keep the scope of the lesson manageable. I always tell teachers to "think big, but start small," especially when it comes to blended learning and technology. It's the coach's job to guide teachers to ensure they maintain a manageable focus and experiment with one model or one piece of technology at time.

For example, a teacher just beginning to use the Whole Group Rotation model, in which the whole class rotates between online and offline activities together, may not want to pull individual students for one-on-one conferencing sessions the first time this model is used. Instead, the teacher may want to focus her or his energy on circulating around the room as students work online to answer questions that arise or troubleshoot technology hiccups.

Similarly, teachers may want to have all students do the same work online the first few times they use the Whole Group Rotation model instead of attempting to design different online activities for students at different levels. Differentiating learning is another layer of complexity that can be added to a lesson when a teacher feels confident planning and facilitating a given blended learning model.

PROVIDE TEMPLATES TO HELP TEACHERS DESIGN BLENDED LESSONS

When possible, create templates that can be reused. The work you do in coaching sessions is most useful when it can be modified and reused for many different lessons. This creates continuity for students because they've seen that pattern before, and it also creates a resource that teachers can use for a future lesson. If teachers know they can reuse and adapt the lessons they've created in your lesson-planning sessions, they'll have more buy-in. It's disheartening to spend an hour or two developing a lesson you can only use once. It's best if that work can help save you time in the future too.

In my last book, *Blended Learning in Action* (Tucker et al., 2016), I explained that it's helpful to think about designing a flipped lesson in three discrete parts, as pictured in Figure 7.1. First, teachers should drive inquiry, pique interest, or assess prior knowledge to create context for the flipped content.

FIGURE 7.1 Flipped Classroom Lesson in Three Steps

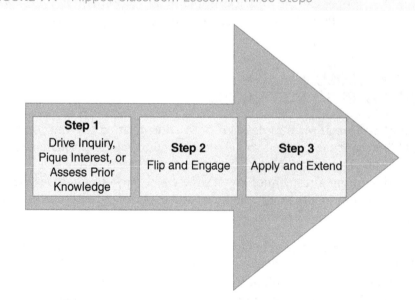

POWER UP BLENDED LEARNING

I recommend this first step happen offline in the classroom. Second, teachers should flip *and* engage students around the online content. If students watch a video on the French invasion of Russia, teachers can wrap that online video in an online discussion that asks them to debate an aspect of the video. Flipping and engaging students online gets them thinking critically about the information. The third step in a flipped lesson—when students apply the new information—takes place in the classroom, where students have access to the subject area expert and a community of peers.

Once teachers have a clear idea of how to plan a flipped lesson, I provide them with a template they can use to lay out the flipped lesson by following this three-step progression. The template visually reminds teachers to follow this flow and prompts them to consider what materials or technology tools they will need for each step and where each step will take place. Will it take place in class, online, or in stations?

Flipped Classroom Lesson Plan Template

Step 1: Inquiry and Exploration Activity description:	What materials or tech tools do you need for this step? Where does this step in the lesson take place (home, class, in stations)?
Step 2: Transfer Information and Engage Activity description:	What materials or tech tools do you need for this step? Where does this step in the lesson take place (home, class, in stations)? How do you assess this step (if desired)?
Step 3: Extend and Apply Activity description:	What materials or tech tools do you need for this step? Where does this step in the lesson take place (home, class, in stations)? How do you assess this step (if desired)?

 Available for download at bit.ly/BLfliptemplate.

Templates provide teachers with a clear strategy they can use when planning a particular type of lesson. They also encourage them to think of the various parts of a blended lesson and consider how those parts fit together.

DON'T JUST PLAN THE LESSON, CREATE IT

Teachers are swamped, so lesson-planning sessions must be hands-on. Instead of simply talking about what a teacher should do, the coaching sessions must be focused on creating all parts of the lesson right then and there.

I was recently coaching an elementary teacher who teaches a combination of first and second graders. Jessica wanted to design a STEM challenge for her students that would allow them to work in small collaborative groups to move through the design process: ask, imagine, plan, create, and improve. My goal was to support her in creating a series of lessons that effectively blended online and offline work to better support students so each group could self-pace through the STEM challenge. The lessons combined videos, discussion, research, sketching, prototyping, and testing.

We met in a small conference room, and Jessica brought the materials she needed to our lesson-planning session. Instead of planning for a single day, we were planning each step of the STEM challenge that would allow students to self-pace through the process of designing and building a bridge. I created a Google Slide presentation and each slide became one step in the design process. I shared the blank Google Slide presentation with her so we were able to work on it together.

At the start of our session, Jessica said, almost to herself, "I'll need to make groups." Then she grabbed her small notepad to make a list of things to do after our session. I stopped her and said, "Let's make the groups now." She hesitated. I explained, "I don't want to send you home with homework. I'd like to get all parts of this lesson done here, so you don't have to take it home and finish it on your own." If she had to go home and create the parts of this STEM challenge on her own, then what was the purpose of our time together?

So Jessica pulled up a list of her students, and I created a slide with a table where she could type in her groups. This way everything—from groups, to directions, to resources—lived in this Google Slide presentation, which she was planning to share with her kids at the start of the STEM challenge. While Jessica delicately arranged big personalities with quieter students into the perfect groups, I added a title and fun background picture of the Golden Gate Bridge to the title slide. I also took her design process and titled each slide with the step it corresponded to in the design challenge. I then began searching for other cool pictures of bridges because we wanted her students to explore and discuss different types of bridges before they began designing their own. These are the little things that nonetheless take time, so I busied myself with these tasks to lighten her load while she worked on groups. I never sit idly in my lesson-planning sessions. This is where I bring value to a coaching relationship. I don't want the teachers I'm working with to feel uncomfortable because I'm just sitting, staring, and waiting for them to finish up whatever task they are on.

One of the long-term goals Jessica and I had established during our initial conversation was to use the Flipped Classroom model to "flip" her instructions by creating short videos of her explaining directions, introducing new ideas, and showing the students how to complete specific tasks. This is a great use of the Flipped Classroom model in an elementary class because it essentially allows the teacher to replicate himself or herself and be in many places at once. As any elementary teacher can attest, kids have a lot of questions. There is only one teacher, so it's helpful to leverage technology to help make sure every student has easy access to information and explanations.

During our session we decided it would be fun for the kids to take photos of their bridges and share them via Google Drive. This would require that they work in pairs using an iPad. One student would hold up a picture and the other student would take a photo of that picture with the iPad and upload it to the class Google Drive account. This is a fairly complex process for first- and second-grade students, so I encouraged Jessica to record a short (less than 1 minute) video tutorial explaining this process. She did not have a video recording device on her computer, so I suggested we use Screencastify, a free Chrome extension. We walked through the process of adding it to her Chrome browser and experimented with it. We did hit a couple of bumps, but they did not deter or disillusion Jessica because I was right there to help her troubleshoot.

There were several moments in this lesson-planning session when Jessica's instinct was to make a note for later—to add to her "to do" list. Each time she reached for her notepad, I said, "Let's do that now." By the end of our 90-minute coaching session, Jessica had a multimedia STEM challenge organized in a shareable Google Slide presentation. I could tell Jessica was relieved that she wasn't leaving our lesson-planning session with more work than she had coming into it.

Teachers should not leave a lesson-planning session with more work than they had coming into it.

REFLECT ON THE ROLE OF TECHNOLOGY IN THE LESSON

As teachers begin to design their blended lessons, it is helpful to build reflection into this process. I realize reflecting on a lesson takes time, but it's helpful if the coach models this for the teacher with the first couple of lessons. Once a lesson is created, think about the aspects of the lesson that use technology. How is that technology being used? Is it merely acting as a substitute for something that can be done offline, or is it allowing students to do something that isn't possible without technology?

Using SAMR (substitution, augmentation, modification, redefinition) as a guide to reflect on how the teacher is using technology can help her or him to better understand the value of technology. Reflecting on the parts of the lesson that incorporate technology and labeling *how* technology is impacting the learning using SAMR, as pictured in Figure 7.2, is a helpful exercise for teachers. If a teacher is simply using technology as a substitute or to augment the learning, then this process of reflecting will highlight that stagnation in technology use. The coach can encourage the teacher to set a new goal that pushes him or her to design a blended lesson that uses technology to modify or redefine the work being done in the classroom.

FIGURE 7.2 Reflect on Technology Use With the SAMR Model

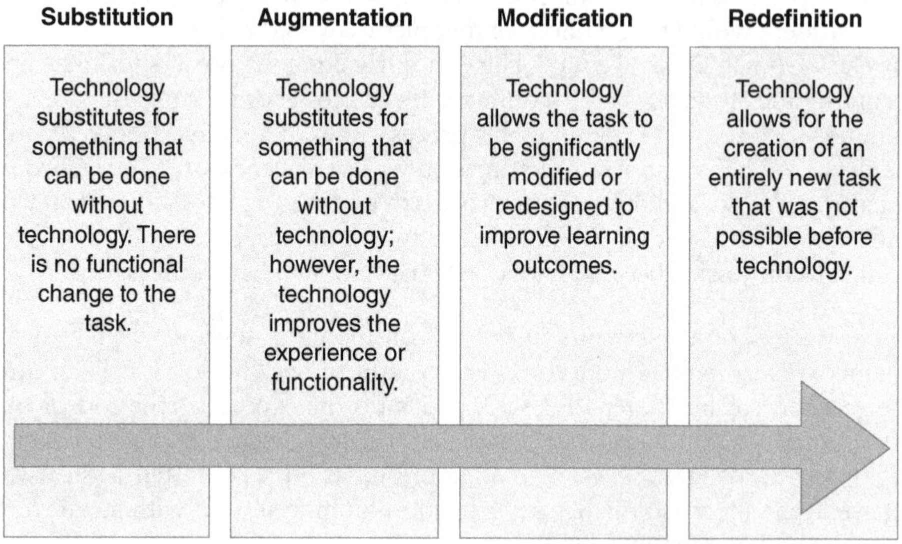

Substitution	Augmentation	Modification	Redefinition
Technology substitutes for something that can be done without technology. There is no functional change to the task.	Technology substitutes for something that can be done without technology; however, the technology improves the experience or functionality.	Technology allows the task to be significantly modified or redesigned to improve learning outcomes.	Technology allows for the creation of an entirely new task that was not possible before technology.

Below are questions you can use with teachers to get them thinking about how they are using technology in their lesson.

- How am I using technology in this lesson?
- Why am I using technology in this lesson?
- How does the technology improve learning for my students?
- What does the technology allow them or me to do that we could not do before?
- Does the technology allow me to individualize or personalize the learning?

- Does the technology allow students to collaborate or create?
- Where would I place this technology use on the SAMR model? Is there a next level that I can imagine to this lesson? Could I use technology to create a totally new task?

This reflection can take the form of an informal discussion or it can be a reflective writing exercise. The key is for teachers to stop, think about the lesson, critique the technology use, and push themselves to think bigger.

DEALING WITH DETAILS

Once the actual lesson is created, it's important to discuss the details that are sometimes overlooked in the initial lesson planning. Below are questions to guide your conversation.

- How will the teacher group students?
- How much time will students have for each task?
- Will students move at their own pace through the lesson or will the teacher need cues to signal transitions?
- What happens if students don't finish their work? Can they take it home? Will there be a homework assignment connected to this lesson?
- If students finish early, will there be next steps or another task they can work on? If so, how will those next steps be communicated to students to keep them on task?

If teachers think through the elements of their blended lesson during planning (see Figure 7.3), they are less likely to hit bumps when implementing because they will have considered these things ahead of time.

FIGURE 7.3 Elements of a Blended Learning Lesson

Grouping students	If teachers are designing lessons that require students to work in groups or move through stations in groups, then they need to consider what type of grouping makes the most sense given the objectives of the lesson. Teachers may want to group students by • skill level, • interest, • strengths in a group dynamic, or • learning preferences. Grouping students strategically can make it easier to tailor instruction and practice for individual students.

(Continued)

FIGURE 7.3 (Continued)

Cues	Cues—visual or auditory—are helpful for moving students from one activity to the next. Teachers will have the most success with a cue if it is consistent. Encourage them to think about what types of activities students will be engaged in and select a cue that will get students' attention and encourage quick transitions. Teachers might want to use • a bell, a snippet of music, or an alarm; • a flash of the lights; or • a projected timer on the front board.
Timing	Depending on the objectives of a lesson and the age of the students, a lesson may be timed by the teacher or self-paced. For example, a teacher facilitating a station rotation at the elementary level may have students spend 20 minutes at each station, then rotate. Alternatively, a secondary teacher might want to consider the benefits of a free-flow station rotation, where students start at a station then move to the next station when they are ready. This gives them more control over the pace of their learning.
Homework	Some teachers give homework and some do not. If you are working with a teacher who regularly gives homework, it's worth talking about the goal of the homework attached to the lesson you've just designed. Perhaps the "homework" would be just the additional time and opportunity students have to finish up the work they started in class. Here are some additional questions to consider: • If the homework is an additional assignment, is it online or offline? If it's online, do all students have access to a device and the internet? If not, will there be an alternative offline activity for them to complete? • How will the homework be presented? Online or in a handout? • Will some class time need to be dedicated to reviewing the expectation for the homework? • Are there resources in place that students can access for support as they complete this assignment on their own?

WRAP UP

Some teachers feel that technology is on pace to replace them. I hear this concern from experienced teachers being asked to shift to blended learning, but I've never worried that technology could replace me. In part, that's because I do not see my primary role in the classroom as a disseminator of information but rather as an architect of learning experiences. If my main job was to be a fountain of knowledge and tell students everything I know about a topic, then technology could definitely replace me. Students can Google just about anything and find answers to their questions, but it takes a talented teacher to design meaningful, interesting, and engaging activities to help students make meaning, think deeply, and create. Therefore, the teacher's role as the designer and architect of learning experiences is invaluable.

Students can Google just about anything and find answers to their questions, but it takes a talented teacher to design meaningful, interesting, and engaging activities to help students make meaning, think deeply, and create.

During the lesson-planning phase of coaching, the coach must help teachers to better understand how to effectively weave together active, engaged learning offline and active, engaged learning online. It is challenging for many teachers to think beyond the whole group lockstep lesson, so providing one-on-one support and lesson templates can make the transition from planning a whole group lesson to a blended lesson easier.

Coaches must also make sure that teachers leave the lesson-planning sessions with a lesson they can use tomorrow. If coaching sessions focus on talking about what teachers "should" do instead of actually planning the various parts of a blended lesson, the teacher is likely to walk away from that time feeling overwhelmed and ill-equipped to design a blended lesson.

BOOK STUDY QUESTIONS

1. How do you plan to communicate with the teachers you coach? What items would you ask your teachers to come to lesson-planning sessions with? Is there anything you need to make sure *you* bring to a lesson-planning session?

2. Are there neutral spaces on campus where you can meet with the teacher to lesson plan? If so, who do you need to contact about using those spaces? Is there a sign-up protocol? How can you articulate the value of meeting in a neutral space to the teachers you are working with?

3. Think about the blended learning model or models your teachers are being asked to use. Design a lesson template to guide your teachers through the creation of a blended lesson for that specific type of model. What steps will teachers need to go through to create a lesson? How can you provide them with structure that supports them as they design their lessons?

4. How can you ensure that your lesson-planning sessions are hands-on and produce a finished lesson? What structure can you bring to the lesson-planning process to help teachers efficiently design the parts of a blended lesson while you are working together? Do you foresee any

challenges to creating the lesson together? If so, what are they and how can you troubleshoot these potential hurdles?

5. This chapter presents a list of lesson-planning details you should discuss with your teacher: grouping strategies, cues, timing, and homework. Is there anything you would add to this list?

6. How will you build in a reflective routine where your teachers evaluate how they are using technology by referencing the SAMR model? What do you think would be beneficial about this reflection? What might be challenging about it? Would you prefer to have a discussion with teachers or have them reflect in writing? If they reflect in writing, would you want them to share that reflection with you? If so, how would you use it?

CHAPTER 8

Coaching: Real-Time Coaching

Too often PD is a pre-planned event and not a process.

—Stacy Hawthorne (@StacyHaw),
online programs director for the
Davidson Academy and educational strategist

INTRODUCTION

Real-time coaching transforms a lesson into an opportunity to learn. The classroom becomes a space where the teacher is encouraged to question, experiment, and reflect. Trust and respect between the coach and teacher are essential to this step in the coaching cycle.

Coaches can use the "pause, discuss, adjust" strategy to guide the teacher in thinking critically about the parts of the lesson and how students are responding to it. Then the teacher can pivot, adjust, and improve the lesson as it unfolds. The "pause, discuss, adjust" strategy allows the coach to highlight what is working well in the lesson and help teachers make minor modifications to improve the lesson.

In addition to the "pause, discuss, adjust" strategy, teachers benefit from written feedback they can use to drive their reflections after the lesson. This chapter will highlight the TNTP Blended Core Teaching Rubric, but there are several different rubrics available to help coaches give thorough feedback quickly and consistently.

This chapter will:

- Encourage coaches to establish norms for real-time coaching

- Introduce the "pause, discuss, adjust" strategy

- Promote the use of a rubric for providing structured feedback on a blended lesson

- Highlight the benefits of documenting the parts of the lesson

PRE-LESSON CHAT: REVIEW LESSON AND ESTABLISH NORMS FOR REAL-TIME COACHING

Before a real-time coaching session begins, it's important to discuss the lesson itself. The coach may not have co-created the lesson with the teacher, so this conversation gives the teacher an opportunity to explain what will be happening in the lesson. Teachers will typically jump right into an explanation of the actual tasks, so it's important for the coach to ask additional questions about the lesson, such as the following:

- What are the objectives of the lesson?

- What skills will students be learning or practicing in the lesson?

- Which blended learning model has the teacher selected for this lesson? How will this model help the students to achieve the stated objectives or allow the teacher to differentiate learning for students at different levels?

- How will the teacher know if students learned what they were supposed to learn or reached the stated objectives?

- What would a successful lesson look like? How will the teacher measure success? Will any data or work be collected?

- How does this particular lesson help the teacher work toward his or her SMART goals?

These questions can guide deeper thinking about the purpose, design, and outcomes of the lesson. The teacher's answers to these questions may also lead to some last-minute changes that improve the lesson or highlight an area of need that the teacher and coach may want to focus on in their next lesson-planning session.

Once the coach and teacher have discussed the lesson, it's time to establish norms for the real-time coaching session. This will put the teacher at ease because she or he will know what to expect during the lesson. The three topics the coach should cover with the teacher before the lesson are pictured in Figure 8.1.

FIGURE 8.1 Establishing Real-Time Coaching Norms

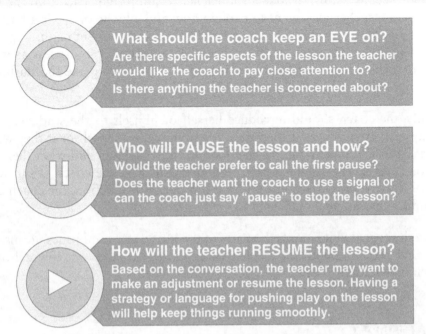

What should the coach keep an EYE on?
Are there specific aspects of the lesson the teacher would like the coach to pay close attention to? Is there anything the teacher is concerned about?

Who will PAUSE the lesson and how?
Would the teacher prefer to call the first pause? Does the teacher want the coach to use a signal or can the coach just say "pause" to stop the lesson?

How will the teacher RESUME the lesson?
Based on the conversation, the teacher may want to make an adjustment or resume the lesson. Having a strategy or language for pushing play on the lesson will help keep things running smoothly.

The coach should begin by asking the teacher if there is anything in particular he or she wants the coach to look for or keep an eye on. For example, the teacher may be worried about using consistent language to manage devices during offline tasks or moments when the teacher is talking. So the teacher might ask the coach to make sure she or he is using consistent verbal cues, such as, "Eyes on me and go 45 degrees." When students tilt their Chromebooks or laptop screens to a 45-degree angle, they can focus on the teacher's instructions instead of being distracted by what is on their screens.

Other teachers may want the coach to look for and identify moments in the lesson when students could work collaboratively in pairs or small groups. The shift from teacher-focused to student-centered lessons can be challenging, so looking for moments or opportunities to allow students to discuss, problem-solve, and work together is important.

Next, the coach should ask the teacher if he or she has a preference about who pauses the lesson for the first time. Some teachers may feel more comfortable initiating the first pause, while others might prefer for the coach to take the lead on pausing the lesson. It's important to ask if there are moments in the lesson when the teacher would prefer *not* to pause it. This allows the teacher to decide what he or she is most comfortable with. Choice and voice are key to building trust between the coach and teacher, ultimately making the real-time coaching a more productive and positive experience for everyone.

It's also helpful to discuss a routine or language to use for resuming a lesson. It might feel awkward at first for a teacher to jump right back into the lesson, so the teacher may want to explain how and why he or she is adjusting the lesson. This way students understand how an adjustment might improve their learning experience. This includes the students in the process as well. Other teachers may just want to clap and say "play" to make the start and stop more fun. It's totally up to the teacher.

Finally, the coach should introduce herself or himself to the students, so I always ask my teachers if they want me to introduce myself or if they want to take the lead on explaining why I am in the classroom and what the goal of coaching is. The students need to understand who the coach is and why she or he is in the classroom. Without a proper introduction, the coach can become a distraction.

Once the coach understands the parts of the lesson and establishes norms for real-time coaching with the teacher, both parties are ready for the real-time coaching session to begin.

REAL-TIME COACHING: "PAUSE, DISCUSS, ADJUST"

When a coach is in the classroom observing and providing feedback on a lesson, he or she can see and hear things that the teacher cannot. Instead of waiting until a lesson is over to ask questions or provide suggestions for improvement, the strategy of pausing a lesson creates an opportunity for the teacher and coach to pause, discuss, and adjust the lesson as it is happening.

Teaching Channel (2018) published a great video titled *Making Learning Public Through Teacher Time-Outs* that demonstrates the strategy of pausing a lesson to engage in conversation about what's happening in the classroom. In the video, Kristin Grey, a K–5 math specialist, explains that during a teacher time-out the "lead teacher or another adult in the room can pause instruction [or a lesson] and either ask a question or have a wondering about the structure of what's happening." The use of the word *wondering* is brilliant in this context. Educators tend to be curious. Teachers may feel like something in the lesson isn't working the way they had hoped. Pausing a lesson gives them the time and space to wonder out loud, bounce ideas around with the coach, and make an adjustment. The term *teacher time-out* was coined by Teresa Lind, a math coach from Lakeridge Elementary School in Seattle, Washington. I love this strategy, but I don't love the name. A *time-out* has a negative connotation in the world of school and adolescence. As a coach introducing this strategy, I always refer to it as "pausing" the lesson. I want students to think of these moments as brief and positive opportunities to learn.

In the Teaching Channel video, an elementary teacher explains a math concept to students sitting on a rug. Instead of just a single coach, there are also a couple of other teachers observing, asking questions, and providing suggestions in real time. The students understand that this coaching session is designed to help their teacher improve the lesson. The goal is to make learning public. Instead of learning being isolated to the student experience, students realize that their teachers are also learning. This can have a powerful impact on the culture of learning at a school because learning happens at every level.

Prior to real-time coaching, I make sure the teacher I am working with understands the purpose and value of the "pause, discuss, adjust" sequence. It's also important to share the "pause, discuss, adjust" strategy with students at the start of the class so they are not surprised or confused when you pause the lesson to discuss it.

I want teachers to know that they are welcome to pause the lesson at any moment to ask a question, make an observation, or wonder about something happening in the classroom. I also provide sentence starters, as pictured in Figure 8.2 under the "Discuss" section, to get teachers thinking about how they might phrase their question or "wondering" when they pause a lesson. It's important that they use constructive language in these moments since students are listening to and learning from these conversations. Finally, I emphasize the power of using the lesson itself as a learning opportunity. Instead of waiting until after a lesson to think critically about what happened, these real-time coaching sessions encourage teachers to be nimble and think about what is happening and make the necessary changes in the moment.

FIGURE 8.2 Real-Time Coaching Strategy: "Pause, Discuss, Adjust"

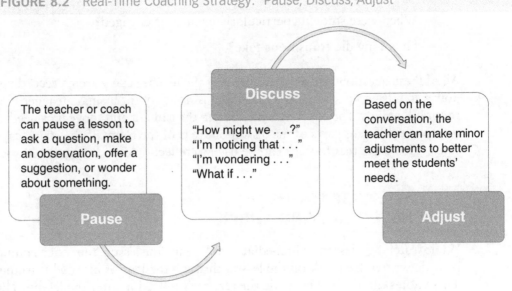

The teacher or coach can pause a lesson to ask a question, make an observation, offer a suggestion, or wonder about something.

Pause

Discuss

"How might we . . .?"
"I'm noticing that . . ."
"I'm wondering . . ."
"What if . . ."

Based on the conversation, the teacher can make minor adjustments to better meet the students' needs.

Adjust

As teachers engage in this practice of "pausing, discussing, and adjusting" a lesson with a coach and then later with the members of their PLC teacher team, they will begin to ask themselves questions about what they are seeing as they facilitate lessons.

- How are students responding to the lesson?
- What are they struggling with?
- When are students most engaged?
- Are students using different approaches to accomplish the same task?
- How is the technology allowing differentiation or personalization?
- Do students have enough time and/or support to complete tasks?

This process of observing and questioning will be invaluable to teachers as they use blended learning models and incorporate technology to gain a better understanding of what works and what doesn't.

DOCUMENT THE PARTS OF THE LESSON

Capturing a lesson or parts of a lesson on film allows the teacher to see the lesson after the fact. While facilitating the lesson, the teacher's attention may be on a single student or group of students for a period of time. This makes it challenging to notice what else is happening in the room, and teachers might find it difficult to answer the following questions:

- Where is there confusion?
- When were students off task?
- When were students particularly excited or engaged?
- How long did transitions take?

All of these questions are easy to answer if the teacher can watch a recording; however, setting up a camera and filming is not easy for a single teacher in a room full of kids. The coach can help set up the camera and move it as needed to capture different parts of the lesson or areas of the room. If the coach captures video clips, that footage can be used to reflect on and discuss the lesson.

WRITTEN FEEDBACK USING
A BLENDED LEARNING RUBRIC

While watching a lesson or immediately following the lesson, the coach should provide written feedback on the lesson through the lens of blended learning. These notes can be used to guide the teacher's reflection after the lesson. The more clear and consistent the notes, the more useful they will be. If a coach uses a rubric to provide a structured evaluation, then it's easier to track the teacher's development over time. Using a rubric also creates clear categories with language describing the levels of mastery for each criterion. This provides the teacher with a clear roadmap of what she or he is working toward.

The TNTP Blended Core Teaching Rubric is a great resource for streamlining a coach's written feedback on a blended lesson because it assesses teacher performance across five performance areas: culture of learning, essential content, academic ownership, demonstration of learning, and student agency.

FIGURE 8.3 TNTP Blended Core Teaching Rubric Performance Areas

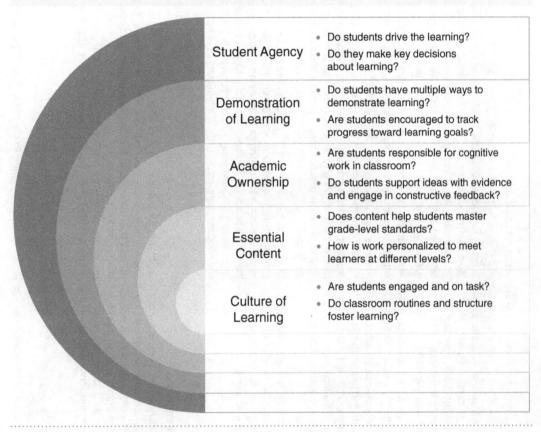

Student Agency	• Do students drive the learning? • Do they make key decisions about learning?
Demonstration of Learning	• Do students have multiple ways to demonstrate learning? • Are students encouraged to track progress toward learning goals?
Academic Ownership	• Are students responsible for cognitive work in classroom? • Do students support ideas with evidence and engage in constructive feedback?
Essential Content	• Does content help students master grade-level standards? • How is work personalized to meet learners at different levels?
Culture of Learning	• Are students engaged and on task? • Do classroom routines and structure foster learning?

Each of the five elements pictured in Figure 8.3 is assessed using a 5-point rubric that describes 1 as "ineffective," 2 as "minimally effective," 3 as "developing," 4 as "proficient," and 5 as "skillful." The rubric describes what each element looks like for each level, so a coach does not need to take copious notes. Instead, the coach can circle the language on the rubric that corresponds to what he or she is seeing in the classroom. Any additional notes can be made in the margin.

Figure 8.4 on the next page shows the "Culture of Learning" performance area of the TNTP Blended Core Teaching Rubric. There is a rubric for each of the five performance areas. A coach may choose to focus on one or two elements during a coaching session instead of tackling all five. In fact, narrowing

FIGURE 8.4 Culture of Learning Performance Area Rubric

CULTURE OF LEARNING: Are all students engaged in the work of the lesson from start to finish?

1. INEFFECTIVE	2. MINIMALLY EFFECTIVE	3. DEVELOPING	4. PROFICIENT	5. SKILLFUL
Very few or no students complete instructional tasks, volunteer responses and/or ask appropriate questions.	Some students complete instructional tasks, volunteer responses and/or ask appropriate questions.	Most students complete instructional tasks, volunteer responses and/or ask appropriate questions.	All or almost all students complete instructional tasks, volunteer responses and/or ask appropriate questions.	All descriptors for Level 4 are met, and at least one of the following types of evidence is demonstrated:
Very few or no students follow behavioral expectations and/ or directions.	Some students follow behavioral expectations and/or directions.	Most students follow behavioral expectations and/or directions.	All or almost all students follow behavioral expectations and/or directions.	Students assume responsibility for routines and procedures and
Students do not execute transitions, routines and procedures in an orderly manner.	Students execute transitions, routines and procedures in an orderly and efficient manner only some of the time and/or require substantial direction from the teacher.	Students execute transitions, routines and procedures in an orderly and efficient manner most of the time, though they may require some direction from the teacher.	Students execute transitions, routines and procedures in an orderly and efficient manner with minimal direction or narration from the teacher.	execute them in an orderly, efficient and self-directed manner, requiring no direction or narration from the teacher.
Students are left without work to do for a significant portion of the class period.	Students are idle while waiting for the teacher or left with nothing to do for one or two minutes at a time.	Students are idle for short periods of time (less than one minute at a time) while waiting for the teacher to provide directions, when finishing assigned work early, or during transitions.	Class has a quick pace and students are engaged in the work of the lesson from start to finish. Students who finish assigned work early engage in meaningful learning without interrupting other students' learning.	Students demonstrate a sense of ownership of behavioral expectations by holding each other accountable for meeting them.

Core Teacher Skills

Maintaining High Behavior Expectations

- Providing specific, concrete, sequential, and observable directions for behavior and academics.
- Addressing all negative and off-task student behavior immediately and in a way that does not slow or disrupt the momentum of each lesson and/or station.
- Issuing logical and appropriate consequences as needed without hesitation, such that consequences are successful in changing student behavior.
- Using voice and presence to maintain authority and convey caring for students.
- Investing time in knowing individual students and in forming relationships to best support their learning.
- Developing an active interest in students' well-being and demonstrating that interest through his/her engagement with students.

Maximizing Instructional Time

- Using efficient techniques for starting and ending lessons.
- Using efficient routines and procedures.
- Planning for and providing work for students to "say yes to" and using strategies to maintain a quick pace throughout the lesson.

Source: TNTP Core Teaching Rubric. Used with permission.

the focus of feedback can make a coaching session more productive and less overwhelming for the teacher. The coach may want to select the rubric that is in line with the SMART goal(s) being focused on in that moment.

If a coach is going to use a rubric like the TNTP Blended Core Teaching Rubric, she or he should introduce this rubric during the lesson-planning step in the coaching cycle. Just as students benefit from seeing the rubric a teacher will use to assess a paper or project, a teacher designing a blended lesson will benefit from knowing what a strong lesson looks like in terms of these five performance areas. It's unrealistic to expect a teacher who is new to blended learning to have a clear vision of what these elements of a lesson should look like in practice. By sharing and discussing the rubric while designing a lesson, the coach creates total transparency about the elements of the lesson he or she will be evaluating and providing feedback on.

Another fantastic resource worth checking out as a possible feedback tool for coaches is the Highlander Institute Blended Learning Best Practices Walkthrough Tool (see Figure 8.5 on the next page). It begins with a section in which the coach can note the devices used, the number of students, the hardware and software used, and the lesson objectives.

NOTES

_____

_____

_____

_____

_____

_____

_____

_____

_____

_____

_____

_____

_____

_____

_____

_____

_____

_____

_____

HIGHLANDER
INSTITUTE
Leveling the Field for All Learners

Highlander Institute Blended Learning Best Practices Walkthrough Tool

Observer:	Teacher(s):	Grade:
School:	Number of students in class:	District:

Available hardware: Circle and write number of units

Chromebook _____ IPad _____ Macbook _____ Smartboard _____

Doc Cam _____ Classroom PCs _____ Other (fill-in) _____ and _____

Duration of class period: _____ Number of support staff: _____

Hardware being used during observation: _____

Software being used during the observation: _____

Lesson Objective: _____

Source: © Highlander Institute (2018) | www.highlanderinstitute.org. Used with permission.

Below the basic inventory of the room and lesson description, the Highlander Institute tool lists four domains that the coach can provide feedback on: classroom culture, student voice and choice, pacing, and self-directed learning. Within each domain are indicators, as pictured in Figure 8.6, and the coach can provide a rating from "There is no evidence of this" to "There is a great deal of evidence of this." Similar to the TNTP Blended Core Teaching Rubric, this tool can simplify the process of providing structured feedback and tracking teacher progress over time.

FIGURE 8.6 Highlander Institute Blended Learning Best Practices Walkthrough Tool—Part 2

HIGHLANDER
INSTITUTE
Leveling the Field for All Learners

Priority Practices Tool Domains and Indicators

DOMAIN	PRACTICE	
Classroom Culture	1A	Tasks are supported by clear instructions
	1B	Students' behavior is appropriate for the task
	1C	Transitions between activities are efficient
	1D	Systems are in place to assist students in solving problems independently
	IE	Interactions between students are positive and productive
	1F	Interactions between students and teachers are positive and productive
	1G	Students have the opportunity to provide input and feedback on learning experiences
	1H	Students are collaborating
Identity, Interest, Agency	2A	Physical classroom environment reflects a wide range of diverse experiences
	2B	Students have choice over how they learn
	2C	Students have choice over what they learn
	2D	Students have choices in how they demonstrate their understanding
	2E	Students set goals for their learning tasks
	2F	Teacher creates connections between the subject matter and student's identity
	2G	Teacher encourages student ownership of learning
Differentiation	3A	Small group instruction is differentiated based on students' needs
	3B	Tasks are differentiated based on students' needs
	3C	Teacher uses a variety of techniques to assess student progress toward learning goals

(Continued)

FIGURE 8.6 (Continued)

DOMAIN	PRACTICE	
	3D	Teacher provides opportunities for students to reflect on their own data
	3E	Teacher uses data to inform instruction
	3F	The classroom experience allows students to progress through learning tasks or content without waiting for the teacher
Rigor and Mastery	4A	Students are given the opportunity to apply learning from one task to another
	4B	Students present evidence that supports their thinking
	4C	Students design or create a product to demonstrate their understanding
	4D	Students are engaged in work that is authentic
	4E	Students are engaged in work that requires higher order thinking skills
	4F	Feedback process is kind, specific and helpful
	4G	Teacher provides students with a clear vision of what mastery looks like

DOMAIN	PRACTICE		STRATEGY
Classroom Culture	1A	Tasks are supported by clear instructions	1A.1 Each station or task has clear instructions posted
			1A.2 Instructions are accessible to students of all languages and reading abilities represented in the classroom
			1A.3 Instructions are concise with few grammatical errors
			1A.4 Instructions reach a variety of learning modalities (e.g., in words, pictures, read aloud)
			1A.5 Students can complete the task based on the instructions given
			1A.6 Other Evidence of Indicator
	1B	Students' behavior is appropriate for the task	1B.1 Teacher provides students with visuals that help them monitor their own behavior
			1B.2 Student behavior is consistent with expressed expectations for a task (e.g., volume level, engagement level, what we should see, anchor chart)
			1B.3 Students are working consistently on assigned tasks
			1B.4 Other Evidence of Indicator
	1C	Transitions between activities are efficient	1C.1 Teacher provides students with visual and auditory cues about where, when, and how they should move
			1C.2 Students transition from task to task safely and efficiently (as instructed)
			1C.3 Teacher provides tools that helps students manage time (e.g., stopwatch, time warning)
			1C.4 Other Evidence of Indicator

DOMAIN	PRACTICE		STRATEGY
	1D	System are in palace to assist students in solving	1D.1 Students have a method to follow if a arise (e.g., re-read directions, ask a neighbor, ask a teacher, parking lot)
			1D.2 Students can use instructions to solve problems
			1D.3 Visuals in classroom support systems in place
			1D.4 Systems are student-friendly and easily accessed (e.g., labeled accessible areas/bins for materials)
			1D.5 Students play a role in the running of classroom logistics
			1D.6 Other Evidence of Indicator
	1E	Interactions between students are positive productive	1E.1 Students communicate using positive language and a level tone with each other
			1E.2 Students adhere to classroom rules and expectations with respect to each other
			1E.3 Students utilize accountable talk stems with each other
			1E.4 Students help each other
			1E.5 Students do not interrupt when peers are speaking
			1E.6 Teacher facilitates problem solving between students
			1E.7 Teacher models and reinforces positive and productive interactions
			1E.8 Other Evidence of Indicator
	1F	Interactions between students and teachers are positive and productive	1F.1 The teacher communicates with students using positive language and a level tone
			1F.2 Teacher reinforces classroom rules and expectations
			1F.3 Teacher adheres to classroom rules and expectations
			1F.4 Students communicate with the teacher using positive language and a level tone
			1F.5 Students adhere to classroom rules and expectations with respect to the teacher
			1F.6 Students positive interactions with adults are recognized and reinforced
			1F.7 Teacher fosters an environment where failure is embraced as part the learning process
			1F.8 Other Evidence of Indicator
	1G	Students have the opportunity to provide input and feedback on learning experiences	1G.1 Students have opportunities to provide feedback throughout the class period
			1G.2 Teacher uses student feedback to inform their practice
			1G.3 Teacher uses a portion of the class period to debrief the lesson experience with students
			1G.4 Other Evidence of Indicator

(Continued)

FIGURE 8.6 (Continued)

DOMAIN	PRACTICE	STRATEGY
	1H Students are collaborating	1H.1 Teacher provides opportunities for students to share roles and responsibilities to complete work
		1H.2 Teacher creates accountability systems for all types of role/responsibilities to(e.g., check list, posters, protocols)
		1H.3 Teacher models and debriefs around meta-cognitive skills and traits involved in collaboration
		1H.4 Students are engaging in meaningful collaboration
		1H.5 Students collaborate with an equitable division of work and effort
		1H.6 Other Evidence of Indicator

Source: © Highlander Institute (2018) | www.highlanderinstitute.org. Used with permission.

FIELD NOTES

The final section of the Highlander Institute tool has an entire page titled "Field Notes" for additional comments, observations, and suggestions. Michael Klein, an educational strategy specialist at the Highlander Institute and an experienced teacher, said,

> We've developed a walkthrough tool that articulates the domains and indicators that we think defines effective teaching in a personalized classroom. When I'm observing, I'll take low-inference notes about teacher actions and student actions, timestamp them and tag them in a software we use called Teachboost. From there I'll choose the highest leverage indicator to focus on and think about 1–2 next steps a teacher can take. Then in the debrief meeting we'll reflect on their lesson and share those next steps.

The specific tool the blended learning coach uses to provide formal written notes is not important as long as some format for taking notes is part of every coaching session. It's easy for teachers to get frustrated, so using a tool to track their progress is key to helping them to appreciate their growth over time. These tools can also be used by the teacher teams in the PLC to provide a structured way to observe each other and provide feedback on lessons.

WRAP UP

When athletes are on the field, the coach is there to support and guide them. The coach yells words of encouragement, makes suggestions for improvement, and pulls players aside to talk about their performance. Similarly, a real-time coaching session can transform the classroom into a learning lab where the teacher has the opportunity to "pause, discuss, and adjust" a lesson with the support of the blended learning coach.

Not only does the coach facilitate real-time modifications and improvements, he or she can also help the teacher to document sections of the lesson and provide written feedback on them. When this written feedback is in the form of a blended learning rubric such as the TNTP Blended Core Teaching Rubric or the Highlander Institute Blended Learning Practice Walkthrough Tool, teachers can begin to track their progress, focus on specific aspects of their blended lessons, and appreciate their growth.

BOOK STUDY QUESTIONS

1. What are the benefits and potential challenges of real-time coaching while a lesson is in progress? How can setting norms help to improve this

process? Is there anything you would add to the "pause, discuss, adjust" strategy?

2. How can a coach help make students feel comfortable with the process of real-time coaching? Is there a constructive way to engage student voices in the real-time coaching process?

3. Explore the TNTP Blended Core Teaching Rubric and the Highlander Institute Blended Learning Practice Walkthrough Tool. Would one of these tools be useful for providing structured feedback to teachers? Is there another rubric or resource you plan to use to provide teachers with feedback? How can tools like these be used to track growth over time?

4. What impact could real-time coaching using the "pause, discuss, adjust" strategy have on the student, teacher, and campus culture?

CHAPTER 9

Coaching: Model Lessons and Co-teaching

The teachers who don't think that there is any other way to deliver their content have the hardest time trying anything new. They honestly don't see any need to change or try anything new.

—Tosh McGaughy (@ToshMcGaughy),
digital learning specialist and blended learning coach

INTRODUCTION

The old adage "Seeing is believing" is true. Teachers have a lot of reasons why they think a particular strategy might *not* work with their population of students. It's easy to dispel those concerns when the coach is willing to go into a classroom to lead a model lesson or co-teach. These two elements of a coach's job are important for different reasons.

A model lesson allows the coach to design a strong lesson to serve as an exemplar and introduce new models, strategies, or technology tools. Co-teaching provides support as the teacher experiments with a new blended learning model. In a co-teaching role, the coach acts as a security blanket during implementation so it's less scary to take risks. If the lesson hits a tech bump, the coach can troubleshoot so the lesson doesn't grind to a halt. If the teacher is worried about juggling the online and offline activities, the coach can split the responsibility of facilitating the lesson with the teacher. This lowers the teacher's anxiety about trying something new and improves the probability that implementation will be smooth.

This chapter will:

- Suggest a strategy for designing and teaching model lessons

- Encourage coaches to co-teach

- Highlight how teaching model lessons and co-teaching can combat the implementation dip

DESIGNING AND TEACHING A MODEL LESSON

One of the best ways to help a teacher see the value of a new approach is by designing and teaching a lesson for them to observe. The teacher provides the target standards and learning objectives, but the coach gets to choose the path. Many coaches who have left the classroom miss creating engaging learning experiences for students, so designing model lessons gives them the opportunity to be creative. For example, a coach might want to experiment with the Flex model, which allows for a more personalized learning experience. To accomplish this goal, the coach could design a "choose your own adventure" lesson built on the Flex model. Or, if a coach notices that the teacher uses the board to write out an agenda or directions, the coach could design a lesson using Google Slides or a HyperDoc to demonstrate how online multimedia directions allow students to self-pace through a lesson. Model lessons allow the coach to highlight a new approach or strategy.

This year I had a teacher ask if I would plan and teach a blended math lesson. She told me her kids were working on classifying triangles and quadrilaterals and measuring angles. She wanted me to plan a lesson that allowed them to practice those new skills using the Station Rotation model. I immediately thought, "I'm not a math teacher. That's not in my wheelhouse." But instead of pushing back or saying no, I decided to go for it. I knew it would be a great opportunity for this teacher, who had 30 years of teaching experience, to see something totally different. As I started planning the lesson, I was immediately excited to find creative, collaborative, hands-on activities to get these kids engaging with the math concepts and using math vocabulary.

Ultimately, I designed a three-station rotation that consisted of the following activities:

Station 1: Play Desmos's Polygraph: Basic Quadrilaterals Game

- Students logged into Desmos, which paired them randomly to play this polygraph game, similar to the classic Guess Who? One student selected a quadrilateral from a collection of images on her or his screen. Then that student's partner, who had the exact same collection of images on her or his screen, asked questions using details, description, and math vocabulary to try to figure out which quadrilateral the partner had selected.

Station 2: Play Always, Sometimes, or Never With Shapes

- Students were assigned partners and given a series of statements, such as, "A rhombus is a square." The students had to decide if this statement was always true, sometimes true, or never true. If they said "Always true," then they had to draw a picture showing how it could be true. If they said "Never true," they had to draw a picture of how it could not be true. If they said "Sometimes true," then they had to draw both pictures.

Station 3: Play With Angles

- Students paired up and each person put three strips of colored tape on a small whiteboard. Each student would measure and label one of his or her angles then switch boards and check his or her partner's work. If the measurement was incorrect, the student would erase it and write the correct answer in his or her color whiteboard marker. Students repeated the process until all the angles were properly measured. They counted up the number of angles written in each color marker and the color that appeared most on both boards revealed the winner.

I set up the lesson on a Google Slide presentation that included an overview slide, a slide with each station title, and the word *directions*, which was hyperlinked to a Google Doc with multimedia directions. I knew that the students had no experience navigating a lesson set up this way, but I also wanted to model a strategy this teacher could use in the future. It's so important that coaches model a clear process for both designing and executing a lesson. That way the teacher can easily replicate the strategies used.

It's so important that coaches model a clear process for both designing and executing a lesson.

As the students entered the room, I was aware that the lesson could totally bomb. These kids didn't know me well, and I had not been present for the lessons leading up to this one. Even though I referenced the grade-level standards for math and used resources such as Illustrative Math that are clearly aligned to the standards, I wasn't sure how students would react. Would it be too hard or too easy? I wasn't sure. However, in my role as a coach, I am constantly asking the teachers I work with to step outside of their comfort zones and try new things. I also need to be willing to take risks if I am going to be an effective coach.

MODEL LESSON CHECKLIST

As a coach plans a model lesson, it's helpful to have a checklist to guide that process. Here is the checklist I use when I am planning a model lesson:

- Identify the objectives of the lesson.

- Reference the grade-level standards.

- Select a blended learning model.

- Articulate clear directions.

- Decide if directions will be online, offline, or a combination of the two.

- Create a clear path for students to follow through the lesson (e.g., Step 1, Step 2, etc.).

- Use a cue to help them transition, if needed, through the parts of the lesson (e.g., bell or timer).

- Determine what the students will deliver (e.g., What are the deliverables or products? What can be finished at home?).

- Design next steps for students who finish early.

- Make sure to share the lesson with the teacher prior to the model lesson.

I followed each of these steps when designing my model math lesson.

Identify the Objectives of the Lesson

A lesson can have several objectives, but the teacher should identify the learning objectives for the lesson the coach is designing. In my model math lesson, the teacher I was coaching said she wanted the students to practice classifying triangles and quadrilaterals and measuring angles. In addition to those specific math objectives, I wanted them to learn how to use Desmos, which is an online math resource they had not previously used. I also wanted them to have experience navigating online directions that would allow each group of students a new level of autonomy as they executed the tasks at each station.

Reference the Grade-Level Standards

Once I knew what the learning objectives were for the lesson, I spent time reviewing the grade-level standards for math to make sure the activities I was designing would target those specific standards. I used online resources such as Illustrative Math to help me select activities that were aligned to specific standards. I also read through some blogs written by fifth-grade teachers to see what types of math activities they were using. When designing model lessons, I try to draw on resources that my teachers can use when they are designing their own future lessons, which is why I selected Desmos and used a math activity available on Illustrative Math.

Select a Blended Learning Model

Sometimes a teacher will request that I use a particular model. In the case of my math lesson, the teacher was beginning to experiment with a split-class rotation for math. She had been dividing the class in half and providing direct instruction and modeling for one side of the room while the other side completed independent practice online via Dreambox. Then she would switch groups and repeat her direct instruction for the second group.

When I designed my model lesson, I used a three-station rotation so the teacher could see a slightly different approach. My goal was to demonstrate how technology can be used to engage students, so I selected a Desmos activity that randomly paired students for the polygraph activity. Too often technology is only used for individual practice. It's important for teachers to realize the power of technology for collaboration. Also, I wanted to get students playing a game as they attempted to measure angles because this was a fairly new skill. Play cannot be overrated as a strategy for keeping kids engaged in a tough task.

All of these pieces were important influences in the design of my model lesson. I'd suggest every coach keep these questions in mind as they design lessons:

- Can I highlight a slightly different approach that will push teachers to expand their approach?

- Can I use technology to foster collaboration and get kids working together?

- Do my activities feel like work or play?

- Will kids be excited to engage with the concepts and with each other?

Create a Clear Path

As I constructed my lesson, I decided to use Google Slides to create a path for students to follow through the lesson. That way I could share the slide deck with everyone using a customized bit.ly link that would be easy for the students to type into their browser windows. I created a title slide, an objectives slide, and a slide with three rectangles representing the three stations. Each rectangle on the third slide included the station number, a title (e.g., "Play Always, Sometimes, or Never With Shapes"), and the word *directions*, which was hyperlinked to a Google Doc with multimedia directions, as pictured in Figure 9.1 on the next page. This made transitioning between activities smoother since the slide deck was already pulled up on each computer. Instead of wasting 5 minutes at the start of each station trying to locate directions, students were a click away. It's the coach's job to model a workflow that can be easily replicated.

It's the coach's job to model a workflow that can be easily replicated.

FIGURE 9.1   Station Rotation Lesson Slide Deck Image

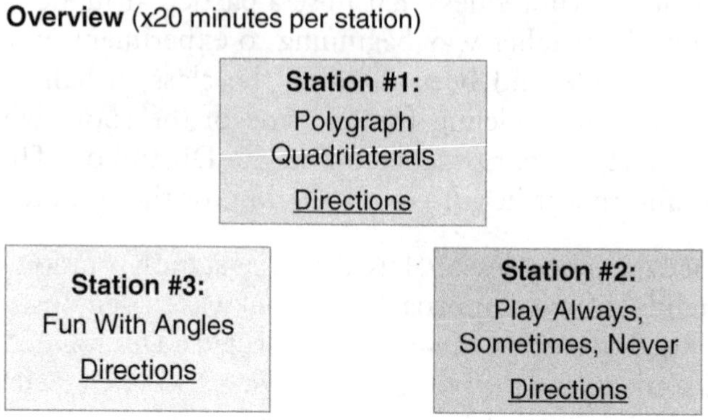

Overview (x20 minutes per station)

Station #1:
Polygraph
Quadrilaterals
Directions

Station #3:		Station #2:
Fun With Angles		Play Always,
		Sometimes, Never
Directions		Directions

Decide on Deliverables

It's crucial to model sustainable teaching practices as the coach leading a model lesson. If I had designed a station rotation with three activities that all produced a deliverable that required feedback, I would have left my teacher with a lot of follow-up work. Too often teachers feel they need to grade everything, which makes designing a lesson with multiple activities, such as a station rotation, daunting. So instead I designed two stations that were grounded in practice and play. Station #1, "Polygraph Quadrilaterals," was an online station where students played a game on Desmos designed to encourage them to use academic vocabulary and think about properties of shapes. It did not require they finish and deliver a product. Station #3, the "Playing With Angles" activity, also didn't culminate in a product that kids had to turn in. The focus for both of these stations was on the process, not on a product.

In contrast to Station #1 and Station #3, Station #2, "Always, Sometimes, Never," did require that pairs of students draw pictures to show how two shapes always, sometimes, or never share similar properties. This was a collaborative and tactile station in which students created a product that could be collected and assessed, or it could simply be used to gauge how much more practice the kids needed on this particular topic.

Design Next Steps

Students work at different paces, so it's important to have an activity for students to focus on if they finish early. This helps to eliminate distractions. I used the last slide on my slide deck to present a math puzzle/brain teaser I found on YummyMath.com. If students were done early, they could try to individually tackle this math challenge. I've also seen teachers post a "What to do if you're done early" list on their board. This can help students to use their time more effectively when they finish an activity before their peers.

Share the Lesson

When I finished my lesson, I shared the slide deck with the teacher. I wanted her to have the opportunity to look through the lesson to make sure I had not designed anything that would be too easy or too challenging. Sharing a lesson in advance can help to put a teacher at ease because she or he knows what to expect.

As students participated in this math lesson, the room filled with their chatter and energy. Kids successfully navigated the parts of each station without needing additional instruction. At one point, the teacher said, "I feel guilty. I'm not doing anything." I pointed out how engaged the kids were and said that I thought the best lessons were the ones when students were driving the learning. I also pointed out that in the future she could use this time to conference with individual students who might need additional support.

When the bell announced it was time to transition to the next station, there were audible groans from students who clearly did not want to move yet because they were enjoying the station they were at. At that point, the teacher commented, "Well, it looks like they are enjoying themselves!" That is how I want every student to feel in class!

Designing and teaching a model lesson makes a blended learning model more accessible and technology less scary for a teacher who is feeling uncertain about the shift to blended learning. The coach has the opportunity to be creative, and the teacher is challenged to consider a different approach to designing and facilitating lessons. Finally, it requires that the coach take a risk, which may in turn lead to the teacher feeling more comfortable being vulnerable and experimenting.

CO-TEACHING

Co-teaching may be the best way to support teachers as they implement new teaching models. In *Leading in a Culture of Change*, Michael Fullan (2007) wrote that "the implementation dip is a dip in performance and confidence as one engages in an innovation that requires new skills and new understandings" (p. 49). Teachers attempting to use new blended learning models and technology will no doubt hit bumps during implementation. Blended learning models require a total shift in the teacher's approach to designing and facilitating lessons. The role of the teacher fundamentally changes when teachers begin to blend online and face-to-face learning experiences. The teacher becomes an architect of learning experiences weaving together learning mediums and a facilitator supporting the learning in class.

It's common for a teacher to leave a targeted training or a lesson-planning session with her or his coach excited to try something new; however, most teachers face this dip in performance and confidence at some point in their blended learning journey. Teachers may experience one of two problems that lead to the implementation dip: "the social psychological fear of change [or] the lack of technical know-how to make the change work" (Fullan, 2007, p. 51).

When a coach co-teaches a lesson, she or he can help to alleviate the fear of change and provide the necessary support needed as teachers attempt to apply their new technical skills.

A NEW TAKE ON CO-TEACHING AT LIBERTY ELEMENTARY SCHOOL

Beginning in September 2016, Liberty Elementary School focused on a co-teaching model designed to provide teachers with cutting-edge technology. Liberty is fortunate to have a multitude of technology, but with everything teachers have to do, it's challenging to learn the new technologies and implement them effectively. As a result, Liberty's SMART Lab was created.

Throughout the year, classroom teachers team up with the Technology Resource Teacher (TRT) and Technology Assistant (TA) to co-teach lessons in the SMART Lab. Each month a new type of technology is introduced. In November, the fifth-grade team was learning about the ocean floor in science and geometry in math, so they used the SMART Lab to learn how to use 3D printing technology, which complemented the curriculum.

During the first lesson, the teacher reviewed the different layers and depths of the ocean floor. After the teacher covered the curriculum, the TRT or TA led a mini-lesson focused on how to use the 3D printing programs so students could design and create 3D models.

As students work, the teacher circulates answering curriculum questions and the Technology Resource Teacher supports the creation of the 3D designs. Prior to this lesson, the classroom teacher had not used the 3D printer, so the SMART Lab provides embedded professional development. The teacher had the opportunity to experience the technology for the first time and have it modeled by the Technology Resource Teacher and Technology Assistant, who are present the entire time.

During the second lesson, the fifth graders created and subdivided plane figures for their geometry unit using 3D printing. At this point, the teacher had the option to request the Technology Resource Teacher be fully engaged or periodically pop in to check on class progress.

After their monthly lessons, teachers are empowered to take their new technology skills and implement them into their classrooms for everyday use. Teachers at Liberty Elementary School learn how to code, 3D print, compose music, make and edit green screen videos, create stop motion films, design video games, and engage in augmented reality applications, among many other technology opportunities.

—*Nichole Thomas (@MrsThomasTRT), technology resource teacher at Liberty Elementary School*

Co-teaching Alleviates the Teacher's Fear of Change

Trying a new teaching method or technology tool can create fear. Teachers like to be the experts, and trying something new and unfamiliar pushes them into the uncomfortable role of being a novice tasked with teaching. It's important for the coach to understand that the teacher is taking a risk and have empathy for the teacher. The dialogic interview strategy discussed in Chapter 4 is designed to create a foundation of trust and openness on which the coaching cycle can build. This strong foundation of mutual respect and understanding becomes particularly important as teachers attempt to implement new strategies. If the coach has established a strong relationship through the initial conversation, observation and debrief, and lesson-planning stages of the coaching cycle, then teachers will feel supported as they implement, especially if the coach is there to co-teach.

I've co-taught whole group rotation lessons where the class transitions between online and offline activities, and my primary job in these lessons is to answer questions, lend support to both the teacher and students, and troubleshoot issues that arise. I'm not actually teaching any content. Instead, I'm simply another adult in the room who can help out as the teacher and students navigate a new type of lesson and/or routine.

Co-teaching Provides Support as Teachers Apply New Technical Skills

Using technology in a lesson requires that teachers both understand how to use the tool and can guide students in using it. Technology can feel like a wild card in a lesson. Often technology tools look different from the teacher's view compared to the students' view, which means students may have questions that the teacher is unsure how to answer. There are also all of the random glitches that can happen when a teacher uses technology—the Wi-Fi might be unreliable or the technology may not work seamlessly on all types of devices. These variables are nerve-wracking for teachers who are not yet confident using technology.

I've co-taught in a station rotation lesson where I led a station that introduced first-grade students to Padlet. In my station they typed a customized bit.ly link into their device to access the Padlet wall, wrote a sentence about their plans for the weekend, and posted a selfie. The goals were to get the kids comfortable typing in links on their Chromebooks and to teach them how to post text and images to a Padlet wall. These were skills we wanted to build on after this lesson, but it was important to lay the groundwork in this station first.

Tips for co-teaching success include the following:

- Follow the teacher's established rules and norms.
- If a student "gets it," encourage him or her to help other students in the room.

- If you hit a bump, model what it looks like to troubleshoot.

- If students have questions and are capable of troubleshooting on their own, allow them to struggle a little. Encourage them to embrace technology to "figure it out" by conducting a Google search or watching a YouTube video if they have access to those tools.

- Model strategies for introducing a lesson and transitioning students through the parts of the lesson.

- Enforce technology norms such as "Go 45 degrees and eyes on me" and "Small screens volume off and screens down."

Co-teaching can help combat the implementation dip by providing teachers with the support that is key to boosting their confidence as they navigate new blended learning models that weave together online and offline.

WRAP UP

Change is scary. Teachers who are tasked with the job of teaching with technology will be nervous about changing their approach to designing, implementing, and facilitating blended lessons. The coach's job is to support teachers as they navigate change by providing strong models that teachers can learn from and attempt to replicate. A model lesson can push teachers to think outside of their box. It can introduce new approaches to designing and facilitating lessons. It allows the teacher to see a blended learning model in action. That concrete example can make this change less scary.

As teachers begin the daunting task of implementing new teaching models and technology tools, coaches can support them by co-teaching lessons. The coach may take a more peripheral role—answering questions and troubleshooting issues with the teacher and students—or may take a more hands-on role actually teaching sections of the lesson with the teacher. It's important to allow the teacher to determine which approach to co-teaching would be most helpful in a given lesson.

Model lessons and co-teaching both help to combat the implementation dip, which happens when people attempt to try a new process or tool. Instead of a teacher becoming frustrated and abandoning a new teaching model or technology tool, which can happen if implementation is rocky, the coach is there to offer support and provide guidance as the teacher navigates the lesson.

BOOK STUDY QUESTIONS

1. Is there anything you would like to add or remove from the model lesson checklist in this chapter? Do you think this checklist would help you design a strong model lesson?

2. What do you perceive as the major benefits of having coaches design and teach model lessons? What might be challenging about designing and facilitating a model lesson? Think about how the coach, teacher, and students might benefit from or struggle with this experience.

3. What should the teacher's role be during a model lesson? Would it be beneficial for the teacher to simply watch, take notes, and use the evaluation rubric mentioned in Chapter 5 to assess the parts of the lesson? What might the benefits and challenges be of using the assessment rubric this way?

4. What factors lead to the implementation dip? How can designing model lessons and co-teaching combat this dip? What can a coach specifically do when working with teachers to ensure they feel supported as they implement new teaching models and technology tools?

5. When should a coach model a lesson versus co-lesson plan or co-teach? When is this strategy most valuable?

6. When a coach is co-teaching, how should she or he decide whether to facilitate on the periphery or take a more hands-on role teaching content? What factors might impact this decision?

7. Are there any additional tips for co-teaching success you would add to the bulleted list in this chapter?

CHAPTER 10

Coaching: Documenting, Reflecting, and Revisiting

As teachers meet with me each month, their growth (as well as challenges and successes) are recorded using Google Forms. This data is used mostly to demonstrate their growth to themselves, as the process can often be overwhelming and daunting; reflection on the journey and celebrations of success are crucial for maintaining momentum and scaling through the schools and the district as a whole.

—Deb Ramm (@Deb_Ramm),
National Board–certified teacher,
instructional technology coordinator, and
PBS lead digital innovator

INTRODUCTION

New trends arise in education, new teaching techniques become vogue, and new technology tools are introduced daily. Educators must carve out time to engage in inquiry and reflection to understand how the lessons they are designing and the technology they are using are impacting students and the quality of their learning.

Blended learning coaches can support teachers in this reflective practice by dedicating time, energy, and space to this process within the coaching cycle. Coaches can help document parts of the lesson and provide structured feedback to guide the teacher's reflection on a lesson. Even though reflection is typically a solitary endeavor, teachers can use technology to reflect on and share their learning so other educators can benefit.

The coach's main responsibility in this final step of the coaching cycle is to help the teacher to use the ideas, questions, and concerns that surfaced during reflection to refine a strategy or modify an approach. From this step, the coach and the teacher may decide to return to an earlier step in the coaching cycle, such as co-lesson planning or co-teaching, to improve on a specific strategy or blended learning model.

This chapter will:

- Emphasize the value of dedicating time to reflection
- Describe the traits of the reflective practitioner
- Highlight the benefits of using documentation to gain an unbiased view of a lesson
- Provide a documentation log to assist the critical analysis of a lesson
- Explore using digital tools to reflect
- Encourage coach and teacher to revisit SMART goals and develop an action plan

DEDICATING TIME, ENERGY, AND SPACE TO REFLECTION

When I work with teachers and facilitate training sessions, I always begin by asking teachers, "What is the most challenging aspect of your job? What makes it hard to teach and reach all students?" I use Mentimeter to collect anonymous teacher responses in the form of a word cloud. The words that appear larger in the word cloud have been submitted by multiple participants. The word cloud pictured in Figure 10.1 was generated by a group of teachers at a blended learning workshop I facilitated over the summer.

FIGURE 10.1 The "Challenges Teachers Face" Word Cloud

Clearly, time is the number one hurdle these particular teachers face in their professional lives. This word cloud is not unusual. Time dominates most of the word clouds I see in my work with teachers. Teachers spend hours outside of class planning lessons and assessing student work. During class most teachers feel they are in a race against the bell to "get through" the curriculum. This leaves many educators feeling exhausted and overwhelmed, so asking teachers to dedicate time each day or each week to reflect may feel like a big ask. However, dedicating time to, investing energy in, and creating space for reflection can lead to meaningful change in a teacher's practice.

The blended learning coach must support a reflective practice by helping the teacher answer the following questions:

- How often will I dedicate time for reflection in my schedule?

- What physical location will be most conducive to reflection?

- How will the practice of reflecting help me to achieve my SMART goals?

- What questions should I ask myself to guide my reflection?

- How do I prefer to reflect and capture my thoughts?

Once teachers have thought about these questions, they should consider scheduling time to reflect in their calendars the same way they block off time for a meeting. Dedicating a window of time to reflection and treating reflective practice as a priority will ensure that it doesn't get neglected.

BECOMING A REFLECTIVE PRACTITIONER

In Barbara Larrivee's (2000) article "Transforming Teaching Practice: Becoming the Critically Reflective Teacher," she described the process of becoming a reflective practitioner as "a personal awareness discovery process" (p. 296). This is not a linear process. Instead, Larrivee identified three practices that are key to becoming a reflective practitioner: making time for solitary reflection, becoming a perpetual problem-solver, and questioning the status quo (see Figure 10.2 on the next page).

These three practices are crucial for a teacher shifting from a traditional teacher-centered classroom to a learner-centered classroom using blended learning models. Teachers shifting to blended learning are constantly trying new approaches that demand thoughtful reflection. Teachers embracing blended learning must question what they are doing, why they are doing it, and how it is impacting students.

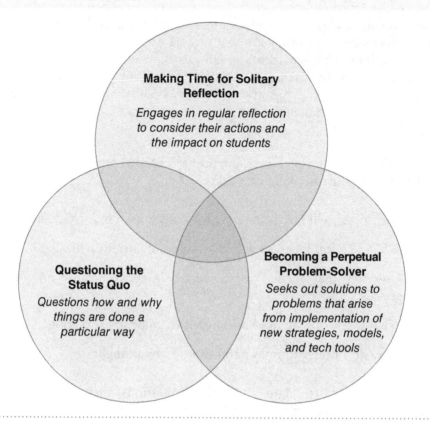

Making Time for Solitary Reflection

There must be consistent reflection on the decisions the teacher is making and on how those decisions impact students. If a teacher is using a particular blended learning model with students, she or he needs to consider why this model will be most effective. The teacher also needs to observe how students respond to this particular model.

Although teachers will engage in solitary reflection, the blended learning coach can help them prepare for their reflective practice by generating questions for teachers to consider as they reflect on a lesson. Below are some general questions, but the coach and teacher may want to brainstorm additional questions specific to a particular lesson or real-time coaching session.

- Why am I doing what I am doing?

- What beliefs about students and learning are driving my decisions?

- How did students respond to a particular model, lesson, or technology tool? Why do I think they reacted this way? What does their reaction tell me or reveal?

- What does the documentation or data tell me about my students' learning and/or progress?
- How can I improve this in future lessons?
- What do I want to make sure I do again because it worked?
- Did this lesson present any management issues that need to be addressed?
- What role did technology play in this lesson? How did technology allow me to differentiate or personalize the learning?
- How can I give students more control over time, place, pace, or path?
- Are there opportunities to give students more agency?

Becoming a Perpetual Problem-Solver

Educators often stress the importance of problem-solving in the context of the classroom. They want students to ask questions, wrestle with challenging situations, and solve problems. However, teachers must also be problem-solvers.

Teachers face many challenges in their work, as evidenced by the word cloud in Figure 10.1. In addition to time, educators who participated in that word cloud activity identified differentiation, ownership, accountability, and parents as challenges they face. Instead of viewing these things as obstacles, educators must think of these challenges as problems to be solved. The problem-solver will think about how blended learning models and technology can be part of the solution.

Teachers concerned with managing a wide range of skill levels in a single class can use technology to do the heavy lifting of differentiation. If students read at significantly different levels, teachers can use adaptive software (e.g., Lexia or Achieve3000) to provide personalized practice or digital curriculum (e.g., StudySync) and online resources (e.g., Newsela or CommonLit) to provide reading at different Lexile levels. If communication with parents is an ongoing challenge, teachers can use Smore to send parents multimedia digital newsletters or create a parent group using Remind to send quick text messages with updates and information.

It's easy to get stuck focusing on all the problems a teacher faces, but the reflective practitioner attacks a problem and actively seeks solutions. According to Larrivee (2000),

A teacher's *modus operandus* should be solving problems, not enforcing preset standards of operation. Problems surface as natural resistance to taking action toward a new possibility. The classroom should be a laboratory for purposeful experimentation. A practice or procedure is never permanent. New insights, understandings, and perspectives bring previous decisions up for reevaluation and consideration. (p. 297)

Instead of teaching the same way he or she was taught, the perpetual problem-solver tries new strategies, examines the impact of these strategies, and makes adjustments. The blended learning coach can assist in this process of brainstorming and designing possible solutions.

Questioning the Status Quo

Just because teachers have used specific strategies in the past does not mean those are the *best* strategies for today's learner. Lecture may have been the most efficient way to teach when there was limited access to information and resources in a classroom; however, today's students have unprecedented access to information and to each other. We need to ask how we can capitalize on student access to information. If students have access to limitless amounts of information, what new skills do they need to develop in order to find, evaluate, analyze, and share that information? How does this access to information change the role of the teacher and the role of the student in the classroom?

Questioning the *why* behind our teaching practices helps us to be open to new ways of teaching and learning. This becomes really important when we consider the best ways to blend technology and tradition. Ultimately, "becoming a reflective practitioner calls teachers to the task of facing deeply rooted personal attitudes concerning human nature, human potential, and human learning. Reflective practitioners challenge assumptions and question existing practices, thereby continuously accessing new lens to view their practice and alter their perspectives" (Larrivee, 2000, p. 296). The shift to blended learning requires that educators challenge assumptions about how students learn and question established practices. The blended learning coach can create a safe space for teachers to embark upon this process of inquiry and reflection.

REFLECT USING DOCUMENTATION

Documenting a lesson and using that documentation to guide reflection can help teachers to avoid seeing only what they want to see in a lesson. Documentation can take many forms: recorded video clips, observation notes and written feedback, work samples, and/or data. The blended learning coach can assist a teacher in collecting documentation from a lesson to be used during reflection.

In Chapter 8 I suggested that the coach set up a camera to record parts of the lesson during a real-time coaching session and provide structured feedback on the lesson using a tool like the TNTP Blended Core Teaching Rubric or the Highlander Institute Blended Learning Practice Walkthrough Tool. These forms of documentation can paint a more complete picture of the lesson and how students responded to it, which provides teachers with details about the lesson that can be closely analyzed to gain a better understanding of what worked and what did not.

If teachers have documentation—be it a video recording, written feedback, student work samples and/or data—from a blended lesson, they can analyze that documentation using a log like the one pictured in Figure 10.3 to gain a better understanding of the lesson and how students responded to it.

FIGURE 10.3 Documentation Log to Help a Teacher Analyze a Blended Lesson

TYPE OF DOCUMENTATION	WHAT DO I NOTICE OR SEE?	WHAT DO I THINK OR WONDER?	WHAT QUESTIONS DO I HAVE?
Video 			
BL coach's feedback 			
Student work samples			
Data 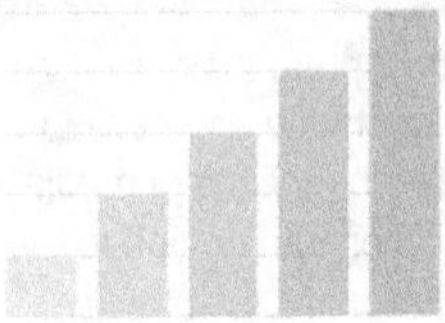			

online resources Available for download at bit.ly/BLDocLog.

A documentation log encourages teachers to look closely at the parts of a lesson and record what they notice. If a teacher is watching a video recording of the lesson, she or he might jot down specific times and describe what she or he or the students are doing in that moment. This can help the teacher to identify moments of high or low engagement as well as instances of confusion. Watching the video may reveal slow transitions or disparities in the time spent with specific groups of students. These small details are hard to catch when the teacher is teaching.

Similarly, looking through student work samples or data generated from online work can help teachers to identify which students are progressing and which students need more support, scaffolding, and practice. This information can help the teacher design a follow-up lesson that better meets the needs of the students.

Finally, analyzing the documentation collected during a lesson prepares the teacher for the actual reflection. He or she will have a much better idea of what worked and what did not. Instead of basing the reflection on the teacher's gut instinct or perception of the lesson, the documentation grounds the reflection in actual evidence and examples.

USING DIGITAL TOOLS TO REFLECT

Reflections can take many forms. Teachers can use a variety of digital tools to capture their reflections; Figure 10.4 provides an overview of a few of these options. It's important that each teacher selects a strategy for reflecting that feels comfortable and natural. Some teachers prefer to keep their reflections private, while others enjoy having an audience and contributing to a larger conversation about blended learning and education.

Teachers who do not enjoy writing will want to explore a different avenue for reflecting, such as sketchnotes, video blogs, or podcasts. Teachers who are given agency in selecting their strategy for reflection are more likely to become reflective practitioners long after their coaching sessions have ended.

FIGURE 10.4 Digital Reflections

TYPE OF REFLECTION	TECHNOLOGY TOOL	FUNCTIONALITY
Online journal	Penzu or Google Documents	Teachers who enjoy writing can capture their reflections online where they are private and easy to revisit. Online journals also allow the mixing of media (e.g., inserting images) so reflection can be tied to the documentation collected in a lesson.
Blog	Wordpress, Blogger	Teachers who enjoy writing and are interested in publishing their reflections for an actual audience can use a blogging platform to reflect on their blended learning journey.

TYPE OF REFLECTION	TECHNOLOGY TOOL	FUNCTIONALITY
Sketchnotes	Google Keep, FiftyThree, Adobe Sketch,	Sketching reflections is a creative alternative for those teachers who aren't inspired to sit down and write or type their reflections. Sketchnotes allow the artist to connect ideas visually. This creative process is ideal for deep reflection.
Audio capture	Voice memos, Voxer	Recording verbal reflections is a quick way to capture a teacher's initial thoughts on a lesson. Teachers can use audio capture apps on their phones and keep them private or join a Voxer group with their blended learning coach and colleagues to share their audio reflections.
Podcast	SoundCloud	For those teachers who want to structure their audio reflections and share them online, podcasts are perfect. They can vary in length depending on the creator and can connect the teacher to an audience.
Video blog	Screencastify, YouTube	Video blogs allow teachers to record their thoughts on a lesson, strategy, blended learning model, or technology tool. This can provide an avenue for teachers to connect with other educators and encourage conversations around the shift to blended learning.

Once a teacher has had a chance to reflect on the lesson, the blended learning coach needs to support the teacher in using the ideas and questions that surfaced during the reflective process to revisit the teacher's SMART goals and refine the approach for future lessons.

REVISIT SMART GOALS

As discussed in Chapter 5, SMART goals should be specific, measurable, attainable, relevant, and timely. When the teacher and coach meet to discuss a real-time coaching session, model lesson, or co-teaching session, it's helpful to have the SMART goals document open so it's easy to reference and update. These SMART goals provide a starting point for the coach and teacher as they discuss a lesson. Instead of talking about every aspect of the lesson, they can focus on the parts of the lesson that relate to the teacher's goals. What does the documentation reveal about the effectiveness of the lesson?

If the coach used the TNTP Blended Core Teaching Rubric or the Highlander Institute Blended Learning Best Practices Walkthrough Tool to provide more structured feedback on a lesson, the teacher and coach can review this feedback in relation to the teacher's SMART goals. The teacher should have an opportunity to ask questions about feedback and work with the coach to develop strategies for improving the lesson and making progress toward his or her SMART goals.

Although reflection is a solitary experience, it's important that the teacher and coach have time set aside to talk about what surfaced during the reflective process. The coach should be the sounding board for the teacher's questions, concerns, or ideas. This will ensure that the reflective process leads to action.

NEXT STEPS: DEVELOPING AN ACTION PLAN

The process of analyzing documentation, reflecting on a lesson, and revisiting SMART goals will inevitably lead to ideas for modification and improvement. This presents a perfect opportunity for the teacher and coach to articulate a revised SMART goal to focus on in subsequent lessons.

Figure 10.5 shows a simple action plan that the blended learning coach and teacher can use to state a revised SMART goal, articulate the action steps needed to accomplish that goal, identify the support needed to accomplish the goal, and propose a timeline for reaching the revised goal. Capturing this information in a collaborative document makes it easy to revisit, edit, and revise as the teacher works.

FIGURE 10.5 Action Plan

REVISED **SMART** GOALS	ACTION STEPS TO ACCOMPLISH GOAL	SUPPORT NEEDED TO ACCOMPLISH GOAL	TIMELINE FOR REACHING GOAL

 Available for download at bit.ly/BLPlan.

POWER UP BLENDED LEARNING

Instead of simply having a conversation about a lesson and the teacher's thoughts on that lesson, the action plan motivates the teacher and coach to put what was learned during the reflection into action. This keeps the teacher thinking about how to improve his or her practice instead of reverting to past comfortable habits.

WRAP UP

Time is a luxury most teachers don't have. Despite being a critical step in the learning process, reflection is often neglected in favor of more pressing tasks. However, teachers shifting to blended learning and experimenting with new types of technology must stop to consider what they are doing, why they are doing it, and how what they are doing is impacting students.

Blended learning coaches must emphasize the importance of being a reflective practitioner and encourage teachers to block off time on their calendars for reflection. Coaches can provide teachers with questions to guide their reflections and options for how they can reflect using digital tools. Coaches can capture documentation during lessons for the teacher to use later to drive both analysis of and reflection on the lesson. After the analysis and reflection are complete, the coach can help the teacher take the ideas and questions that surfaced to create an action plan that is specific and tied to a clear timeline. This helps the teacher to continue progressing on her or his blended learning journey.

BOOK STUDY QUESTIONS

1. How can coaches help teachers dedicate time to reflection? Develop and practice a 1-minute elevator pitch that clearly states the value of reflection as part of a teacher's practice.

2. Are there additional practices you would add to the list of those that are crucial to being a reflective practitioner? What might be challenging about making time for solitary reflection, becoming a perpetual problem-solver, and questioning the status quo? How can a coach help teachers to mitigate these challenges?

3. Are there other forms of reflection and corresponding digital tools that you would add to Figure 10.4? What are the benefits of sharing a reflection with a larger audience via a blog, video blog, or podcast?

4. How will analyzing documentation from a blended lesson and completing a documentation log benefit the teacher? What impact will this

process have on her or his reflection and action plan? What is the danger of reflecting on a lesson without any form of documentation? What types of documentation might be most useful?

5. How can the habit of revisiting SMART goals and articulating action plans help teachers as they shift to blended learning?

CHAPTER 11

School Community Leaders & Coaches

Virtual Coaching

The benefit of the video coaching is that teachers and coaches can see into classrooms across the district and learn from each other. They get to reflect on their own practice and get insight on what is happening in other teachers' classrooms.

—Anne Atherton (@AnneAtherton27),
eLearning coordinator

INTRODUCTION

The two biggest challenges associated with adopting a coaching culture to support a shift to blended learning are scalability and financial investment. First, finding qualified instructional experts with blended learning expertise, dynamic coaching skills, and a temperament conducive to coaching is a challenge. Individuals who fit this profile may be scarce in a district looking to shift to blended learning.

Second, the cost of scaling a coaching program to ensure that a single coach does not have too many teacher contacts to be effective is a challenge. Too often districts will employ a handful of "coaches" who are tasked with supporting hundreds of teachers throughout an entire district. This results in coaches who are unable to provide the one-on-one support necessary to be effective, which in turn translates into frustration on the part of the coaches, who feel they cannot offer the support they know teachers need. This negatively affects teachers as well because they are not able to access the coaching they need to shift to a blended learning model.

Virtual coaching may offer a solution for districts that believe in coaching as a critical part of their professional development plan but are facing both personnel and budget challenges. Just as blended learning models leverage the power of technology to meet the needs of a diverse group of teachers, virtual coaching can offer an avenue for coaches all over the country to get inside classrooms, lesson plan with teachers, and provide meaningful feedback to guide a transition to blended learning.

This chapter will:

- Identify challenges with scaling and funding real-time coaching
- Highlight the benefits and limitations of virtual coaching
- Recommend technology tools useful for virtual coaching
- Describe how a virtual coach can follow the coaching cycle using online communication and collaboration tools

REAL-TIME COACHING: CHALLENGES OF SCALE

A meta-analysis of coaching programs published by Harvard University, Kraft, Blazer, and Hogan (2017) identified two challenges associated with scaling a high-quality coaching program: (1) finding and retaining skilled coaches and (2) the substantial cost of funding a high-quality coaching program.

In their report, Kraft et al. (2017) concluded by stating that "traditional on-site coaching programs are a resource-intensive intervention simply due to the high personnel costs of staffing a skilled coaching corps." Despite this challenge, however, they highlighted web-based virtual coaching as a potential new approach for pairing teachers with coaches all over the nation. This approach to scaling coaching by leveraging the power of online tools makes intuitive sense for blended learning given that the goal of blended learning is to weave together online and offline learning for students. Perhaps the best way to show teachers the value of this is to use virtual coaching or a mix of virtual and real-time coaching with teachers transitioning to blended learning.

Kraft et al. (2017) noted the potential benefits of using virtual coaching to address the challenges associated with scaling a one-on-one coaching model. They asserted that "leveraging video-based technology can lower coaching costs by eliminating commute time and increasing the number of teachers with whom an individual coach can work." For districts with limited resources or with locations that make connecting teachers with skilled experts a challenge, virtual coaching may be the most cost-effective approach for embracing a coaching culture. In contrast to employing a handful of full-time coaches on-site who may not have the expertise needed to be effective in the role of a blended learning coach, virtual coaching "has the potential to increase access to high-quality coaches for schools or districts without local expertise," allowing coaches with specialized training from all over the globe to work with teachers online (Kraft et al., 2017). Often schools pay high speaking and travel fees to fly experts to a physical location for a single day of training; however, that money may be better spent investing in virtual coaches who can work with teachers for a couple of hours every week over the course of a month, semester, or school year.

Kraft et al. (2017) also pointed out that having an on-site coach who provides feedback can cause teacher anxiety and job insecurity. Working with a virtual coach who is physically removed from the school has the potential to "reduce possible reservations among teachers about mixing PD and evaluator roles by having their coach be both physically separate from and unaffiliated with their school" (Kraft et al., 2017). Lower levels of anxiety can translate into a more productive coaching relationship.

THE POWER OF CLOUD COACHING

In 2010 I moved away from my home in Florida and my school, Grandview, where I had been teaching since 2001. Though I left Grandview's geographical proximity, I remained in a leadership role from 2010 to 2012, serving as academic dean and teacher. In this capacity I explored the power of one-on-one and small group online coaching, both for teacher professional development and for personalizing learning for students. Even in 2010 technology held the power to make this distant form of coaching feel up close and personal with video and real-time interactions.

Ongoing coaching provides critical support as follow-up to the more conventional PD workshops, which spark interest but fall short of helping teachers internalize new learning and work through inevitable challenges. I had been using a coaching model while on-site at Grandview as it allowed me to engage with teachers in a much more personalized and co-creative manner in the design of their professional growth plans. When I moved to "the cloud" I utilized tools like Google Apps for Education (now G Suite) to chat in real time and collaborate on documents with teachers. Through Skype, not only could I observe a class but I could capture a much more authentic experience as students were not always aware of my presence. While meeting with teachers face-to-face was also still valuable, it was easy to see the potential of virtual coaching, especially as I was often able to offer assistance "on demand" through chat and discussion board notifications.

I took this blended coaching model into my subsequent school leadership roles (even though I was not working remotely) and into my role as a part-time blended learning coach. Now at Learning Innovation Catalyst (LINC), we are

(Continued)

(Continued)

expanding this blended coaching model to help scale what has previously been a cost-prohibitive and human resource–taxing model of professional development. It's exciting to see the goal of ongoing learning, teacher support, and iterative application of new learning come to life through this blended model!

—Tiffany Wycoff
@TeachOnTheEdge

BLENDED OFFLINE AND ONLINE COACHING IN LARGE DISTRICTS

Some school districts are so large that the virtual coach may actually be an individual employed by the district who uses a blended approach to coaching so he or she can support teachers at a variety of school sites, thus spending less time traveling from place to place and more time actually coaching. A coach in this position can truly blend the coaching experience by mixing face-to-face coaching sessions with virtual sessions.

For these coaches using a blended approach to coaching, it is most effective to go through the full coaching cycle once in person and then shift to virtual coaching. This allows the coach to establish an in-person relationship with the teacher she or he is coaching and then build on that with virtual coaching sessions. This also makes it easier for coaching to be more sustained if a teacher needs support over a longer period of time.

This type of coaching allows for a "gradual release" approach to supporting teachers. The coach can begin in a hands-on role with in-person conversations, observations, lesson-planning sessions, etc. and then transition into an online support role. For example, once a teacher has developed confidence in her or his ability to plan a blended lesson, the coach can shift that step in the coaching cycle online. Instead of teacher and coach planning a lesson side by side in the conference room, the teacher can begin to plan blended lessons using a collaborative document with a lesson template and the coach can leave comments and suggestions for the teacher to help improve the design of the lesson and use of technology.

BENEFITS AND LIMITATIONS OF VIRTUAL COACHING

Coaching, at its core, is about building relationships. For some that is definitely easier to do face-to-face, while for others meaningful relationships can be formed online. The key for a virtual coach is to use dynamic online tools that allow for communication, collaboration, co-creation, and reflection to execute each step in the coaching cycle. It may be tempting to bypass an observation or initial conversation using the dialogic interview format and dive right into recording videos and providing feedback. However, those initial steps in the coaching cycle are crucial to forming a connection with the teachers we are working with.

There will be times when a coach feels the limitations of not actually sitting in a classroom. It can be harder to get a feel for the room, the students, levels of engagement, and so forth when you are watching a video. But many of these gaps can be filled when the coach and teacher debrief to discuss specific aspects of the lesson after it has concluded and the coach has had an opportunity to watch the video of the lesson. In fact, having video documentation to review when talking about specific moments in a lesson or when referencing interactions between students and the teacher, their peers, or the content may actually help to highlight what is working and what isn't in a blended classroom. As any teacher can attest, it is almost impossible to observe and remember every aspect of a lesson.

VIRTUAL SPIN ON THE COACHING CYCLE

Coaches can execute the various steps of the coaching cycle virtually using collaborative tools, online conferencing software, and video recordings.

FIGURE 11.1 Virtual Blended Learning Coaching Cycle

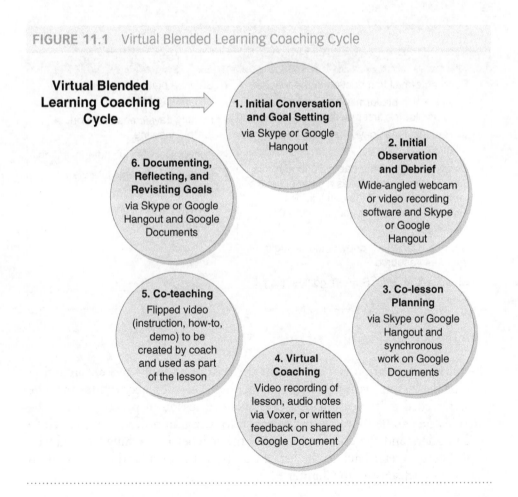

Initial Conversation and Goal Setting

This first meeting is important because it sets the tone for coaching. It may be tempting to skip the conversation and goal-setting session, but this virtual meeting is crucial to establishing a relationship between coach and teacher. The coach should communicate directly with the teacher via e-mail to establish the platform they will use for this first meeting. Google Hangout or Skype work well for this purpose. If the virtual coach plans to use the dialogic interview format, it can be helpful to send a description of the interview along with questions to the teacher ahead of time so he or she understands the format of the conversation. The coach will also want to share an editable version of the SMART goal–setting document with the teacher so the teacher can take a look at it prior to the first meeting. The teacher may even want to jot some ideas down on this document prior to the meeting.

Figure 11.2 identifies the specific tasks the coach and teacher should complete prior to the initial conversation and goal-setting meeting to ensure it is as successful as possible.

FIGURE 11.2   Coach and Teacher To-Do List for Initial Conversation and Goal Setting

COACH'S TO-DO LIST	TEACHER'S TO-DO LIST

• Send an e-mail introduction to the teacher.
  ○ Ask which platform is easiest for teacher to use for the first meeting.
  ○ Request times/days that work best to meet.
• Send a Google Calendar invitation for this first meeting that includes a clear objective for the meeting and a video link or instructions for how to join the virtual meeting.
• Share a "Can View" copy of the dialogic interview resource.
• Share a "Can Edit" SMART goal–setting document.
	• Select a platform for the first virtual meeting.
	• Identify days/times that work best for this meeting.
	• Accept Google Calendar invitation.
	• Review the dialogic interview resource.
	• Review SMART goal–setting document.

Initial Observation and Debrief

The initial observation is a chance for the coach to see the teacher in action prior to the lesson-planning stage in coaching. This step necessitates that the teacher record a "typical" lesson or a blended lesson in practice. Then the video lesson can be shared with the coach to watch in order for the coach to better understand the context in which the teacher is teaching. It might be helpful here to refer back to the list of questions to consider during an initial observation (discussed in Chapter 6):

- How is technology being used? What curricula, programs, technology tools, and/or online resources are currently in use?

- How is the room set up? Do students sit in small groups, pairs, or rows? Who is the focus—the teacher or the students?

- What is a typical lesson like? What are kids doing? How varied are the activities? How often do they rotate from one activity to another? How are transitions handled?

- How engaged are students in their learning? Do they seem interested in the activities and on task? How much autonomy do they enjoy?

- Do students have opportunities to control the pace of their learning?

- What is the teacher's primary role in the classroom? What is the student's primary role?

The more accurate the coach's view of the classroom, the more effective the coach will be at ensuring the coaching sessions will be context specific and focused on distinct models and technology tools that will benefit the teacher and students most.

Figure 11.3 identifies the specific tasks the coach and teacher should complete prior to the initial observation and debrief to ensure this step is as successful as possible.

FIGURE 11.3 Coach and Teacher To-Do List for Initial Observation and Debrief

COACH'S TO-DO LIST	TEACHER'S TO-DO LIST
• Identify what video recording tools the teacher has access to.	• Select a video recording tool (see Figure 11.8) to use for your observation.
• Provide guidance for how to record the lesson in the form of a how-to video tutorial, a practice run-through, or written directions.	• Identify a location in the classroom from which to record or ask a colleague to record your lesson.
• Create a Google Calendar event for this observation with the goals of the observation clearly stated in the description.	• Set up video recording prior to the lesson you plan to record.
• Make a copy of the initial observation notes Google Doc and share it as a "Can Comment" document with your teacher.	• Review the initial observation notes resource. • Upload video to Google Drive or YouTube and share it.
• Select debrief questions from Chapter 6 to use in your follow-up conversation.	• Share your video with your coach (or link to your video) and write a brief e-mail providing the context for the recorded lesson.
• Review your teacher's SMART goal–setting document prior to your debrief.	

Co-lesson Planning

Co-lesson planning is best when done synchronously, or at the same time. For this planning session, the coach and teacher should use Skype or Google Hangout *and* a shared online document such as Google Docs or OneDrive. Both Skype and Google Hangout establish a human connection, enable easy brainstorming, and allow for screen sharing. These pieces are crucial to continuing to build a relationship but also make practical sense by allowing the coach to walk the teacher through online resources or tools. I love to sketch out lesson concepts on a whiteboard, which is also easy to share visually if I use a video communication tool.

The coach and teacher will also want to work synchronously on a shared document as they create the lesson. As I emphasized in Chapter 7, it's crucial to create the parts of the lesson together instead of simply talking about what the teacher should do. The more productive these lesson-planning sessions, the more willing the teacher will be to invest time and energy into this coaching process.

Figure 11.4 identifies the specific tasks the coach and teacher should complete prior to the lesson-planning session to ensure it is as successful as possible.

FIGURE 11.4   Coach and Teacher To-Do List for Co-lesson Planning

COACH'S TO-DO LIST	TEACHER'S TO-DO LIST

• E-mail the teacher prior to the planning session to remind him or her of what to "bring" or have on hand to ensure the session is productive.
 	
• Create a Google Calendar event for this lesson-planning session and share it with your teacher.
 	
• Come to the lesson-planning session with lesson templates to support the planning process.
 	
• Review the SMART goal–setting document.
 	
• Pull up the overview of the SAMR model to use as a reference.
	• Bring the materials requested by the coach to the lesson-planning session.
	
	• Accept Google Calendar invitation.
	
	• Be prepared to fill the coach in on the following:
	  ○ What do you want to cover in the lesson we are designing today? What are the learning objectives?
	  ○ Which blended learning model do you want to use for this lesson?
	  ○ Do you have an idea of how you'd like to use technology in this lesson?
	
	• Come prepared to create.

Virtual Coaching

Virtual coaching is the step in the coaching cycle that is most different from real-time coaching. In the classroom a coach can press "pause" on a lesson and highlight different aspects of the lesson or note student engagement. When coaching is done virtually, that feedback comes after the lesson has already taken place.

Some companies offer a "bug-in-ear" approach to virtual coaching that allows a coach located remotely to observe a teacher's lesson and provide feedback through an earpiece. Proponents of this approach have stated this strategy "enables a teacher to make better decisions, rescue a shaky lesson, and learn as he or she teaches" (Rock, Zigmond, Gregg, & Gable, 2011). My concern with this approach is its potential to be distracting for the teacher delivering the lesson. Wearing a headset and listening to instructions while also juggling the demands of teaching may be overwhelming. This bug-in-ear method also requires a significant financial investment in the equipment used.

A simpler approach to virtual coaching is to have the teacher record a lesson or parts of a lesson and share that video recording with the coach just as she or he did for the initial observation. Then the coach can watch the video and provide detailed feedback on the parts of the lesson through the lens of the ISTE Standards or using resources such as the TNTP Blended Core Teaching Rubric or Highlander Institute Blended Learning Practice Walkthrough Tool.

Feedback can take the form of written notes with timestamps that correspond to specific moments in the video or audio notes. An app such as Voxer can be used for this. Audio notes have the advantage of allowing the teacher to hear the coach's tone, which may make those notes more meaningful to the teacher as compared to written notes. Ultimately, the format of the feedback should take the form that the coach and teacher agree would be most valuable.

After the notes have been delivered, it's important to have a follow-up conversation about the lesson to review the highlights, discuss adjustments, and allow the teacher to ask questions. The sooner the coach can deliver the feedback and schedule this follow-up conversation, the better. The more time that goes by between the lesson and the feedback, the less useful or relevant the feedback will feel.

Figure 11.5 identifies the specific tasks the coach and teacher should complete prior to virtual coaching to ensure this coaching is as successful as possible.

FIGURE 11.5 Coach and Teacher To-Do List for Virtual Coaching

COACH'S TO-DO LIST	TEACHER'S TO-DO LIST
• E-mail teacher prior to the virtual coaching session to confirm a date and describe the process you will use to provide feedback on the lesson.	• Accept Google Calendar invitations.
	• Design a blended lesson or use the lesson you created in your lesson-planning session.
• Create three Google Calendar events: ○ Event 1: The day the teacher will deliver the recorded lesson ○ Event 2: The day you will deliver your feedback on the lesson ○ Event 3: The day you and your teacher will meet for the follow-up discussion	• Select a video recording tool (see Figure 11.8).
	• Identify a location in the classroom from which to record or ask a colleague to record your lesson.
	• Set up video recording prior to the lesson you plan to record.

(Continued)

FIGURE 11.5 (Continued)

COACH'S TO-DO LIST	TEACHER'S TO-DO LIST
• Watch the recorded lesson and provide detailed written or recorded audio feedback using the ISTE Standards and blended learning hallmarks as your lenses (see Chapter 8). • Share the notes with your teacher via a shared document for written notes or an app like Voxer for audio notes. • Make note of the highlights, adjustments, and questions you want to use to guide your follow-up conversation.	• Upload the video to Google Drive or YouTube and share it. • Share your video with your coach (or link to your video) and write a brief e-mail providing the context for the recorded lesson. • As you read through or listen to the coach's feedback, make note of any questions you have or things you want to discuss further in the follow-up conversation.

Co-teaching

Co-teaching is the element of the coaching cycle that some virtual coaches may decide not to include in their work with teachers given that they cannot physically be in the classroom. However, I'd argue that this step in the cycle opens the door for a creative use of the Flipped Classroom model. I'm a big advocate of using blended learning models when we train teachers on blended learning, so this is an opportunity for the coach to create a flipped video to teach content, walk students through a new technology routine, or provide a how-to tutorial. The coach can demonstrate what a strong video looks like and highlight strategies for engaging students around online content. Instead of simply creating a video, the coach can build a dynamic online experience for students using the Flipped Classroom model that will complement the work the teacher is doing. If the coach does not want to create her or his own content, she or he can use high-quality videos available online (e.g., at TED-Ed, Khan Academy, or YouTube) to create a flipped lesson. In addition to providing a model for how to leverage the Flipped Classroom model, the coach is supporting the teacher and taking something off the teacher's plate. This can help the teacher feel that the coach is a real partner in this process.

Figure 11.6 identifies the specific tasks the coach and teacher should complete prior to the co-teaching session to ensure the session is as successful as possible.

FIGURE 11.6 Coach and Teacher To-Do List for Co-teaching

COACH'S TO-DO LIST	TEACHER'S TO-DO LIST
• E-mail the teacher to set up a video chat. • Create a Google Calendar event for the video chat.	• Accept Google Calendar invitation. • Decide which lesson you would like support from your coach in the form of a flipped lesson.

COACH'S TO-DO LIST	TEACHER'S TO-DO LIST

• Meet virtually with the teacher to discuss the goals of the lesson and see how you can support that work with a flipped lesson.
 	
• Design a dynamic flipped classroom lesson that engages students around video content online.
 	
• Deliver the video and any student directions needed to navigate the flipped lesson to the teacher at least 24 hours prior to the lesson.
	• Design the parts of the lesson you will teach or facilitate.
	
	• Review the flipped lesson.
	
	  ○ Do you have any questions or need clarification on any part of the lesson?
	
	  ○ Do any adjustments need to be made prior to the actual lesson?

Documenting, Reflecting, and Revisiting Goals

During virtual coaching, everything is documented—from the video recordings to the feedback—so the coach can focus on supporting the teacher as she or he reflects, revisits goals, and refines strategies and lessons.

In preparation for the follow-up meeting, teachers can analyze the documentation to capture observations, ideas, and questions to help guide this final coaching session. Then the coach and teacher can work synchronously on the action plan document to revise the teacher's SMART goals and refine a particular strategy or model to prepare for a future lesson.

Figure 11.7 identifies the specific tasks the coach and teacher should complete before the meeting on documenting, reflecting, and revisiting goals to ensure this meeting is as successful as possible.

FIGURE 11.7 Coach and Teacher To-Do List for Documenting, Reflecting, and Revisiting Goals

COACH'S TO-DO LIST	TEACHER'S TO-DO LIST

• E-mail the teacher to set up a video chat.
 	
• Create a Google Calendar event for the video chat.
 	
• Review SMART goal–setting document.
 	
• Review feedback on the lesson to be discussed.
 	
• Share a copy of the documentation log so the teacher can analyze the lesson in preparation for this conversation.
 	
• Generate some reflective questions specific to the lesson to guide the teacher's reflection.
 	
• Make a copy of the action plan document and share it with your teacher.
	• Accept Google Calendar invitation.
	
	• Analyze the documentation from the lesson and use the documentation log to capture observations, ideas, and questions.
	
	• Decide on a strategy for reflecting:
	
	  ○ What type of reflection (online journal, blog, video blog, sketchnotes, etc.) will you do?
	
	  ○ When and where do you plan on reflecting?
	
	  ○ Will you block off time in your calendar to get this done?

TECHNOLOGY TOOLBOX
FOR VIRTUAL COACHING

The specific tools a coach and teacher use are not as important as the functionality that is necessary to execute the various parts of the coaching cycle. Below are some technology tools worth checking out. Ultimately, the tools a virtual coach uses will depend on the devices and funding available to both the coach and teacher.

FIGURE 11.8 Technology Tools Perfect for Virtual Coaching

Communication	Skype Google Hangouts FaceTime Zoom Voxer
Collaboration	Google Drive OneDrive Dropbox
Documentation	Swivl Screencastify QuickTime Edthena

STAYING ORGANIZED
WITH GOOGLE CALENDAR

A shared Google Calendar can be a virtual coach's best friend because it allows for easy scheduling and communication between the coach and teacher. For a virtual coach juggling several online interactions, it's helpful to create events in a Google Calendar that clearly identify the focus of the coaching session; create a Google Hangout video call link or provide information for another online meeting tool, such as Skype; and invite the "guest" or teacher directly from the Google Calendar event.

It can be challenging for a virtual coach to keep track of all the various parts of the coaching cycle, especially when the coach is working with multiple teachers. Sometimes those teachers are even in different time zones, which can complicate scheduling further. Using Google Calendar strategically, as pictured in Figure 11.9, to color code events, provide clear instructions, and communicate effectively with teachers can eliminate miscommunication and help to avoid missing important delivery dates. Being reliable is paramount as a virtual coach. It's crucial to keep your scheduled appointments with your teacher to avoid feelings of frustration, which can damage the relationship you've built together.

FIGURE 11.9 Using Google Calendar Strategically for Virtual Coaching

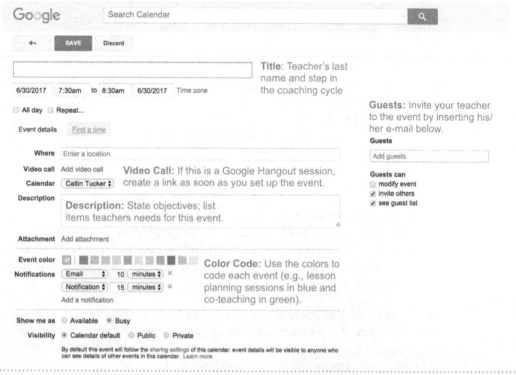

Source: **Google Calendar.**

WRAP UP

Virtual coaching can help to mitigate the personnel and financial challenges of bringing a high-quality coaching program to scale in a large district or a district located in a remote location. Even coaches on-site at a school can use a blended approach to coaching, mixing face-to-face sessions with online coaching for more flexibility.

Virtual coaches can use the wealth of online communication, collaboration, and documentation tools to replicate the blended learning coaching cycle online. Even steps in the coaching cycle that seem nearly impossible to accomplish remotely, such as co-teaching, can be executed by using blended learning models like Flipped Classroom. If the coach and teacher are committed to working together, the virtual coach can model the effectiveness of using technology to teach and learn. This can be a powerful experience for a teacher attempting to use technology with students.

BOOK STUDY QUESTIONS

1. Does your district currently use any virtual coaching or online training? If so, what form has this online training taken? How successful has it been in supporting teachers as they shift to blended learning?

2. This chapter identifies some of the benefits and challenges of virtual coaching as compared to in-person coaching. Are there any additional benefits and/or challenges you would expect to encounter with virtual coaching? How can any challenges you identify be mitigated?

3. What tools would you use to communicate, collaborate, and document work? How would the tools you have access to impact your ability to execute the virtual blended learning coaching cycle?

4. Particular steps in the virtual blended learning coaching cycle, such as co-teaching, may be more challenging to carry out. Which other steps might be hard to accomplish and why? How can you use technology to overcome these challenges? What is the value in going through the whole coaching cycle and not skipping steps?

5. In this chapter I suggested using Google Calendar strategically to stay organized. Are there other technology tools or apps that you plan to use when working with your teachers? If so, what are they and how will they improve your virtual coaching experience?

CHAPTER 12

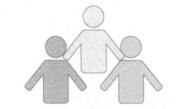

School Community Leaders & Coaches

Professional Learning Communities

The value of a PLC is determined by the clarity of vision in an organization; the commitment of its members to learn, take action, and reflect; and the structures and practices in place to support (not impede) working towards this vision. As the value of any of these variables declines, so does the function of a PLC.

—Ivy Ewell-Eldridge (@IEwellEldridge),
trainer and literacy content specialist

INTRODUCTION

Although many educators think of a professional learning community (PLC) as a team of teachers that meets regularly to plan, a PLC is a campus-wide commitment to learning. PLCs are designed to build inquiry, collaboration, action, and iteration into the school schedule to cultivate a culture of learning on a campus. The power of the PLC was articulated by John Hattie, who synthesized over 800 meta-analyses on the factors that impact student achievement. As quoted in DuFour (2009), Hattie concluded

> that the best way to improve schools was to organize teachers into collaborative teams that clarify what each student must learn and the indicators of learning the team will track, to gather evidence of that learning on an ongoing basis, and to analyze the results together so that they could learn which instructional strategies were working and which were not.

Ultimately, student success depends on the school's ability to become a learning organization committed to continual improvement and innovation.

Schools that believe blended learning will yield higher levels of engagement, improve learning outcomes for students, and provide more personalized learning opportunities must be committed to supporting teachers as they learn how to use blended learning models and technology. This can only be accomplished if teachers are encouraged to continue learning and looking critically at their practice. Leadership must build time into the school schedule for this or it is unlikely to happen consistently.

Coaching can support a PLC by providing intense one-on-one sessions with teachers as they learn how to plan and implement blended lessons; however, coaching cannot be the end of the conversation. Coaches can only work with so many teachers at one time. The PLC model provides ongoing peer support. Teachers who move through the coaching cycle with a blended learning coach will have a strong foundation on which to build, but the PLC will provide the time and space to continue expanding their practice, refining their skills, and sharing what they've learned with their peers. Coaching will provide teachers with strategies, resources, and tools they can use to support one another as they work together. Ideally, the teachers working in a teacher team will lesson plan together, observe one another and provide non-evaluative feedback, engage in real-time coaching, and reflect on their blended learning journeys together.

WHAT IS A PROFESSIONAL LEARNING COMMUNITY?

In 1998 DuFour and Eaker wrote *Professional Learning Communities at Work: Best Practices for Enhancing Student Achievement*, in which they defined a professional learning community as an "environment that fosters mutual cooperation, emotional support, and personal growth as [teachers] work together to achieve what they cannot accomplish alone" (p. xii). DuFour and Eaker believed all professional learning communities possess six common characteristics:

1. a shared mission, vision, and values;
2. collective inquiry;
3. collaborative teams;
4. an action orientation and experimentation;
5. a commitment to continuous improvement; and
6. a results orientation. (pp. 25–29)

DuFour and Eaker's PLC framework was designed to help schools "build capacity for implementing and sustaining change" (Blankenship &

Ruona, 2007, p. 2), and it emphasized the roles of the various members of a school community, from principal to parents. However, not as much attention was "given to how collaborative teams [would] function and the importance of sharing team learning school-wide" (Blankenship & Ruona, 2007, p. 2). For the purpose of this book, I want to encourage leadership to think about a PLC as "an ongoing process in which educators work collaboratively in recurring cycles of collective inquiry and action research to achieve better results for the students they serve. A PLC operates under the assumption that the key to improved learning for students is continuous job-embedded learning for educators" (All Things PLC, 2018). This definition effectively encapsulates the parts of the professional learning community as described by DuFour, DuFour, Eaker, and Many (2006) in *Learning by Doing: A Handbook for Professional Learning Communities at Work*.

DuFour et al. (2006) emphasized that a PLC is not simply the groups of teachers who meet but rather the larger organization—i.e., the entire school. While DuFour et al. (2006) recognized the teacher teams within a school community as key building blocks within the PLC, they pointed out that "much of the work of a PLC cannot be done by a [teacher] team but instead requires a schoolwide or districtwide effort" (p. 10). A strong PLC will require a vision for change, the appropriate allocation of resources, and continued learning at the highest levels of a school community. Schools committed to blended learning must be willing to invest in learning for both students and teachers. If financial investment ends with hardware, a Wi-Fi infrastructure, and digital curriculum, the flood of technology is more likely to overwhelm teachers than to inspire them to embrace blended learning.

THE PLC PROCESS

The teacher teams within a PLC are not simply meeting to discuss the latest challenges they face or share best practices. They are engaged in an ongoing cycle of inquiry and action. Figure 12.1 on the next page presents the primary steps of the inquiry and action cycle.

DuFour et al. (2006) stated that the goal of a PLC "is not simply to learn a new strategy, but instead to create conditions for a perpetual learning environment in which innovation and experimentation are viewed not as tasks to be accomplished or projects to be completed but as ways of conducting day-to-day business—forever" (p. 13). This cycle of continual learning is crucial for teachers shifting to blended learning. Given how new blended learning is in the realm of education, it makes sense that the PLC process of inquiry and action would be invaluable to the success of a blended learning initiative. Teachers should be encouraged to move through this process as they begin using specific models, strategies, and

FIGURE 12.1 PLC Process of Inquiry and Action

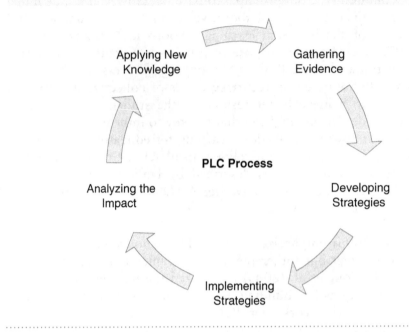

technology tools with students. A shift to blended learning that does not encourage this thoughtful collaborative process is bound to lose sight of the *why* behind the shift away from traditional teaching and learning practices.

I always caution teachers not to use technology for technology's sake. Technology should be used to replace, improve, and innovate. This requires that teachers work together to identify learning objectives and evaluate student strengths and weaknesses at a particular grade level or in a specific subject area. This is accomplished by gathering evidence, discussing that evidence, and deciding how technology and blending learning models can improve learning outcomes for students.

Gather Evidence

During the process of gathering evidence, the team compiles student work and data. The goal is to determine where students are struggling and where they are succeeding. This will inform the work the teachers do and enable them to target specific areas of need. To narrow the focus, teacher teams can select a grade-level content standard to focus on for this inquiry and action cycle and collect work samples and data connected to that specific standard or skill.

FIGURE 12.2   Gathering Evidence

Gather Evidence	Teams:	The team will target:
	• Analyze student work and data • Identify areas of need • Reference standards to better understand the specific skills students should be developing • *Optional*: Use the SMART goals strategy for identifying the team's short-term goals Key Questions: • What are students doing well in terms of standards and skills? • What standards and skills are they struggling with? • Which areas of need are most urgent to address? • Why are students struggling in this particular area? • How are teachers currently teaching this particular standard or skill? • Are any members of the team using technology to help students develop in this particular area? If so, how is tech being used?	

 Available for download at bit.ly/PLCguide.

Develop Strategies

Once an area of need is identified, the team must decide how to best address that need using a specific blended learning model, teaching strategy, and/or technology tool. During the step in the cycle when strategies are developed, teachers will draw on their individual experiences and expertise, their work with the blended learning coach, and additional research and reading on the area of need.

The team must design a lesson or series of lessons to target the need identified. Similar to the lesson-planning session with the blended learning coach, the team should work collaboratively to construct all parts of the lesson during their time together. This will make the time spent in teacher teams more productive and rewarding.

FIGURE 12.3 Developing Strategies

Develop Strategies	Teams:	Lesson Plan:
	• Draw on strategies, blended learning models, and/or technology tools gathered during whole group training with an expert and one-on-one work with a blended learning coach	
	• Develop a clear strategy for meeting the area of need	
	• Design a blended lesson each teacher can use with students	
	• *Optional*: Invite coach into lesson-planning session or share lesson with the coach for feedback prior to the lesson	
	Key Questions:	
	• What do we want students to learn or be able to do? How will we know if students were successful?	
	• What blended learning model will the team use? How will this model best meet the need identified? What is the benefit of this model over others in this particular situation?	
	• How can we support students who struggle during this lesson?	
	• How can technology be used strategically to provide targeted instruction, personalized practice, or opportunities for collaboration?	
	• What will the teacher collect during this lesson that can be used to analyze the impact?	

 Available for download at bit.ly/PLCguide.

Implement Strategies

Each member of the team will implement the lesson he or she designed and collect documentation from that lesson. This documentation will help the teacher team reflect on the success of the lesson in meeting the specific need identified. This documentation, which can consist of video, work samples, performance data, and/or observation notes, will help the team collectively evaluate how students performed during the lesson.

FIGURE 12.4   Implementing Strategies

Implement Strategies	Teams:	Documentation:
	• Implement the lesson designed during their teacher team time • Capture video of the lesson, collect work samples from students, and gather data on student performance and progress • *Optional*: Invite a blended learning coach in to support the lesson, help record sections of the lesson, or capture non-evaluative observation notes Key Questions: • What went well? When did students seem most engaged? • What was challenging? Did students struggle with any aspect of the lesson? Were there any management or technology issues that needed to be addressed? • What types of questions did students ask during the lesson? • Which aspects of their learning did students have control over—time, place, pace, and/or path? Are there opportunities for students to enjoy more control or autonomy in future lessons like this? • What data or information about individual student performance or progress was created during this lesson?	☐ Video ☐ Work samples ☐ Data ☐ Observation notes

 Available for download at bit.ly/PLCguide.

Analyze the Impact

Once the teacher team has implemented the lesson or series of lessons, its members will need to spend time looking at the documentation collected and discussing what that documentation reveals about the lesson. Teacher teams should dedicate time to watching any video clips recorded as a group, looking at the work samples and data, and sharing any observation notes they made during the lesson itself.

Teacher teams should use video footage like a football team uses game film to engage in a post-game analysis. Instead of making assumptions about the lesson or relying solely on student work or the teacher's description of the lesson, the video recordings provide an unbiased window into the lesson. Teachers can see students engaging with each other, the teacher, and the lesson. The teacher team can make observations that might have been impossible for the teacher facilitating the lesson to make in real time. The process of watching video from a lesson can help the team to more effectively identify the areas of strength and weakness in a lesson to better understand its impact. Because the lesson has been created by the group, this analysis should focus on the lesson and the students' engagement.

Once the team has discussed the impact of the lesson, it should articulate some next steps to guide its work moving forward. The team members may decide a follow-up lesson or more practice is required to address the area of need they are focusing on for this inquiry and action cycle. The process of analyzing the lesson's impact may reveal another area of need to be addressed in the next inquiry and action cycle. The team should capture all of those notes to help guide its work in the future.

FIGURE 12.5 Analyzing the Impact

Analyze the Impact	Teams: • Bring student work, artifacts, and/or data to the team to look at and discuss • Take turns sharing a quick synopsis of how the lesson went using questions from the section on implementing strategies to guide this conversation • If video clips were collected, watch and discuss those Key Questions: • What do the student work, artifacts, and/or data reveal about the lesson? • How successful was the lesson at targeting the area of need or the specific standard identified by the team during the section on gathering evidence? • Where are students experiencing success or progress? Do students need additional instruction, scaffolds, or practice? How can these be built into subsequent lessons?	Team Analysis: Next Steps:

 Available for download at bit.ly/PLCguide.

Apply New Knowledge

After analyzing the impact of the lesson, the teacher team will take what it learned and apply this to design the necessary follow-up activities or lessons. The team members may feel that the work they did successfully addressed the need established at the start of the cycle. More likely, however, the process of analyzing the impact will reveal the need for additional scaffolding or practice for some students and next-level work for others. At this point the

FIGURE 12.6 Applying New Knowledge

Apply New Knowledge	Teams:	Lesson Plan:
	• Use the information collected by analyzing the lesson's impact to improve, refine, and redesign the lesson	
	• Design a lesson applying what was learned in this cycle to continue to improve on the blended learning model, teaching strategy, and/or technology tools.	
	• *Optional*: Invite a blended learning coach in to support the team members as they decide which blended learning models and technology tools will work best to help them apply what they've learned and adjust work for students at different levels.	
	Key Questions:	
	• What is the objective of this lesson? What will students walk away knowing or being able to do?	
	• How will we assess the success of this lesson?	
	• How does this lesson accommodate students at different levels of proficiency and mastery? How will this lesson help support students who are still struggling? How will it challenge students who are already proficient?	
	• Will the teacher have time to work with individual students or small groups of students who need additional support? What will other students do while the teacher is working with these students?	
	• How will technology be used to personalize instruction and/or practice for students at different levels?	

 Available for download at bit.ly/PLCguide.

team will need to think about how it can leverage blended learning models and technology to support students who are at different levels of proficiency or mastery.

As a teacher team moves through the cycle of gathering evidence, developing strategies, implementing those strategies, analyzing the lesson's impact, and applying new knowledge (see Figures 12.2–12.6), the blended learning coach can be a valuable resource during the developing and implementing strategies and the applying new knowledge steps in this cycle. The coach can join a teacher team once an area of need has been identified and help its members to consider the best blended learning model and technology tools available to meet that need. Then, as teachers implement, the coach can support individual teachers using the lesson plan designed by the team. This provides opportunities for a blended learning coach to work with a teacher team in addition to his or her work with individual teachers.

In fact, as a teacher team develops, it can incorporate elements of the coaching cycle into its work. While developing strategies, team members can draw on their experiences, templates, and documentation from their lesson-planning sessions with the blended learning coach. Similarly, as teachers implement a strategy, they can document the lesson by recording video that can be viewed with other members of the team to drive non-evaluative feedback. The word *non-evaluative* is important here. Teacher teams will not be successful if the members feel they are being judged or attacked. Like the blended learning coach who works with an individual teacher, the teacher team members must treat their work together as a partnership designed to help each teacher continue learning and improving.

ORGANIZING THE TEACHER TEAMS WITHIN A PLC

Teacher teams within a PLC can be organized by grade level or subject area, or they can be interdisciplinary. However, teams composed of teachers teaching the same grade level or subject area may find it easier to tackle the inquiry and action cycle by designing strategies that can be used easily in all of their classrooms. The documentation collected during the lesson will be easier to analyze as a team because students are completing similar tasks and producing similar products.

Interdisciplinary teams may need to focus on using specific teaching strategies or blended learning models that can be applied to different courses with varied curricula. The artifacts, student work, and data collected by teachers in different disciplines will also be different, which may make it more challenging to identify patterns as the team analyzes the impact of a lesson or strategy.

The size of a teacher team can vary based on the size of a staff and on scheduling challenges, but the teacher teams I've seen that work best together are composed of four to six members. Anything more than that can make collaboration a bit more challenging due to the number of voices in the conversation. Larger teams will need more time to develop strategies and analyze the documentation they've collected after implementation.

Ideally, teacher teams on a campus share a preparation period that encourages daily or weekly meetings. If teacher teams do not have time to meet built into their schedules in the form of a common preparation period, they are less likely to meet and those meetings are more likely to feel like something extra they are being asked to do. The goal of a PLC is to create opportunities for job-embedded learning to occur and build that professional learning into the fabric of the teacher's day. This is best achieved when leadership organizes the master schedule to ensure teacher teams have time to meet during the school day.

WRAP UP

A professional learning community is a schoolwide commitment to professional learning. This job-embedded approach to learning groups teachers into teams that work together to move through a cycle of inquiry and action. The goal is for teachers to identify areas of need, develop strategies to meet those needs, and analyze the impact of those strategies in order to continue improving in their teaching practice and, as a result, improving learning outcomes for students.

The beauty of the PLC is that it prioritizes learning at all levels of a school community. Instead of simply talking about how we can help students to be more successful, the PLC recognizes that teachers must continue to learn if students are going to be successful. It builds time into a teacher's schedule to meet, collaborate, and learn with her or his colleagues. This continued learning is crucial for teachers shifting to blended learning because technology is changing so rapidly. The role of technology in education will continue to alter the landscape of learning. If teachers are going to stay on top of these changes, learning cannot be confined to a handful of professional development days in a year. Schools dedicated to cultivating a culture that values and prioritizes professional learning will be more successful navigating change.

BOOK STUDY QUESTIONS

1. Does your school currently use a PLC to help teachers continue learning and refining their practice? How has the process of inquiry and action in this chapter impacted the way you view the work done in your PLC, if you have one?

2. Review the inquiry and action cycle. Is there anything you would add to this cycle? Which aspects of the cycle might be most challenging for teacher teams? How might leadership and/or blended learning coaches support this process?

3. Think about the steps in the coaching cycle. How might a teacher who has worked with a blended learning coach draw on that experience to support the work being done by his or her teacher team?

4. If you do not currently use a PLC model for professional learning, what challenges might exist in organizing teacher teams? Would you organize them by subject area or grade level, or would your teams need to be interdisciplinary? Can the master schedule be built around these teacher teams to ensure their work is built into their schedule?

5. How might the commitment to building a PLC impact school culture? Do you think teachers on your campus would be receptive to this model?

References

All Things PLC. (2018). *About PLCs*. Solution Tree. Available at http://www.allthing splc.info/about

Blankenship, S. S., & Ruona, W. (2007). *Professional learning communities and communities of practice: A comparison of models, literature review*. University of Georgia. Available at https://files.eric.ed.gov/fulltext/ED504776.pdf

Borko, H., Jacobs, J., & Koellner, K. (2010). Contemporary approaches to teacher professional development. In P. Peterson, R. Tierney, E. Baker, & B. McGaw (Eds.), *International encyclopedia of education* (Vol. 7; pp. 548–556). Oxford: Elsevier.

Boyd, J. (2008). *Coaching in context*. Department of Education and Early Childhood Development. Available at https://www.eduweb.vic.gov.au/edulibrary/public/ teachlearn/student/coachingincontext.pdf

Briggs, S. (2016). Andy Murray: "Ivan is the best coach I've had. It was good to have someone who could normalise failing." *The Telegraph*. Available at https://www.telegraph.co.uk/sport/2016/06/18/andy-murray-ivan-is-the-best-coach-ive-had-it-was-good-to-have-s/

The Christensen Institute. (2018). *Blended learning definitions*. Available at https:// www.christenseninstitute.org/blended-learning-definitions-and-models

Corcoran, T., McVay, S., & Riordan, K. (2003). *Getting it right: The MISE approach to professional development*. Philadelphia, PA: Consortium for Policy Research in Education.

DeMonte, J. (2013). *High-quality professional development for teachers: Supporting teacher training to improve student learning*. The Center for American Progress. Available at https://www.americanprogress.org/issues/education-k-12/ reports/2013/07/15/69592/high-quality-professional-development-for-teachers/

Doran, G. (1981). There's a S.M.A.R.T. way to write management's goals and objectives. *Management Review*, 70(11), 35–36.

DuFour, R. (2009). *Professional learning communities: The key to improved teaching and learning*. Available at http://www.advanc-ed.org/source/ professional-learning-communities-key-improved-teaching-and-learning

DuFour, R., DuFour, R., Eaker, R., & Many, T. (2006). *Learning by doing: A handbook for professional learning communities at work* (2nd ed.). Bloomington, IN: Solution Tree Press.

DuFour, R., & Eaker, R. (1998). *Professional learning communities at work: Best practices for enhancing student achievement*. Alexandria, VA: Association for Supervision and Curriculum Development.

Farber, M. (2017). Google tops Apple as the world's most valuable brand. *Fortune*. Available at http://fortune.com/2017/02/02/google-tops-apple-brand-value

Fullan, M. (2007). *Leading in a culture of change*. San Francisco, CA: John Wiley & Sons, Inc.

Gagnon, S., & Wagner, A. (2016). Acute stress and episodic memory retrieval: Neurobiological mechanisms and behavioral consequences. *Annals of the New York Academy of Sciences, 1369*(2016), 55–75. doi: 10.1111/nyas.12996

Grey, K. (2017). *Making learning public through teacher time-outs*. The Teaching Channel. Available at www.teachingchannel.org/videos/teacher-time-out

Highlander Institute. (2018). Highlander Institute Blended Learning Best Practices Walkthrough Tool. Available at http://fuseri.highlanderinstitute.org/wp-content/uploads/2016/11/External_HighlanderInstituteWalkthroughTool_2016-2017-1.pdf

Horn, M., & Staker, H. (2014). *Blended: Using disruptive innovation to improve schools*. San Francisco, CA: Jossey-Bass.

Joyce, B., & Showers, B. (2002). *Student achievement through staff development*. Alexandria, VA: Association for Supervision and Curriculum Development. Available at http://docplayer.net/10333476-Student-achievement-through-staff-development.html

Knight, J. (2011a). *Unmistakable impact: A partnership approach for dramatically improving instruction*. Thousand Oaks, CA: Sage.

Knight, J. (2011b). What good coaches do. *Educational Leadership, 69*(2), 18–22.

Kraft, M., Blazar, D., & Hogan, D. (2017). The effect of teaching coaching on instruction and achievement: A meta-analysis of the causal evidence. *Review of Educational Research*. Available at https://scholar.harvard.edu/files/mkraft/files/kraft_blazar_hogan_2017_teacher_coaching_meta_analysis_wp.pdf

Larrivee, B. (2000). Transforming teaching practice: Becoming the critically reflective teacher. *Reflective Practice, 1*(3), 293–307. doi: 10.1080/14623940020025561

Maxwell, C. (2016). *A deeper look at the Flex model*. Blended Learning Universe. Available at http://www.blendedlearning.org/a-deeper-look-at-the-flex-model

Meyer, L. (2016). Report: High-functioning professional learning communities support student achievement. *The Journal*. Available at https://thejournal.com/articles/2016/10/24/report-high-functioning-professional-learning-communities-support-student-achievement.aspx

The New Teacher Project. (2016). TNTP Blended Core Teaching Rubric. Available at https://tntp.org/assets/TNTP_Blended_Core_Teaching_Rubric_Fall_2016_Edition_v2.2.pdf

Powell, A., Rabbitt, B., & Kennedy, K. (2014). iNACOL Blended Learning Teacher Competency Framework. *iNACOL*. Available at https://www.inacol.org/wp-content/uploads/2015/02/iNACOL-Blended-Learning-Teacher-Competency-Framework.pdf

Powell, D., Diamond, K., Burchinal, M., & Koehler, M. (2010). Effects of an early literacy professional development intervention on Head Start teachers and children. *Journal of Educational Psychology, 102*(2), 299–312. doi: 10.1037/a0017763

Project Tomorrow. (2013). *Learning in the 21st century: Digital experiences and expectations of tomorrow's teachers*. Available at http://images.email.blackboard.com/Web/BlackboardInc/%7B44fe5cc3-3c7d-4ec0-824b-489b25ca8062%7D_ProjectTomorrow2013_Teacher_Report_Draft.pdf

Rock, M., Zigmond, N., Gregg, M., & Gable, R. (2011). The power of virtual coaching. *Educational Leadership, 69*(2). Available at http://www.ascd.org/publications/educational-leadership/oct11/vol69/num02/The-Power-of-Virtual-Coaching.aspx

Sinek, S. (2011). *Start with why: How great leaders inspire everyone to take action.* New York, NY: Penguin Group.

Sparks, D. (2001). Why change is so challenging for schools. *National Staff Development Council, 22*(3), 42–47.

Sturgis, C. (2017). *How competency-based education differs from the traditional system of education.* iNACOL. Available at https://www.inacol.org/news/how-competency-based-education-differs-from-the-traditional-system-of-education/

Teaching Channel. (2018). *Making learning public through teacher time-outs* [Video]. Available at https://www.teachingchannel.org/videos/teacher-time-out

Thorne, K. (2003). *Blended learning: How to integrate online & traditional learning.* London: Kogan Page Limited.

Tucker, C., Wycoff, T., & Green, J. T. (2016). *Blended learning in action.* Thousand Oaks, CA: Sage.

University of Florida Lastinger Center for Learning, Learning Forward, & Public Impact. (2016). *Coaching for impact: Six pillars to create coaching roles that achieve their potential to improve teaching and learning.* Gainesville: University of Florida Lastinger Center; Oxford, OH: Learning Forward; and Chapel Hill, NC: Public Impact. Available at www.learningforward.org/coaching-for-impact/

Varner, M. (2017). *5 building blocks of an effective brand promise. Workfront.* Available at https://resources.workfront.com/project-management-blog/the-5-building-blocks-of-an-effective-brand-promise

Westergaard, N. (2013). *What's your brand promise?* Brand Driven Digital. Available at http://www.branddrivendigital.com/brand-promise

Yoon, K., Duncan, T., Lee, S., Scarloss, B., & Shapely, K. (2007). *Reviewing the evidence on how teacher professional development affects student achievement.* National Center for Education Evaluation and Regional Assistance. Available at https://ies.ed.gov/ncee/edlabs/regions/southwest/pdf/REL_2007033.pdf

Index

Helping educators make the *greatest impact*

Corwin books represent the latest thinking from some of the most respected experts in K–12 education. We are proud of the breadth and depth of the books we have published and the authors we have partnered with in our mission to better serve educators and students.

SERENA PARISER

This handy guide offers 50 proven best practices for managing today's classroom, complete with just-in-time tools and relatable teacher-to-teacher anecdotes and advice.

GRAVITY GOLDBERG

Can brilliant teaching boil down to five practices? In *Teach Like Yourself*, Gravity Goldberg applies ideas from fields of psychology, education, and science to name five key habits involving core beliefs, practice, relationships, professional growth, and one's whole self.

JOHN ANTONETTI AND TERRI STICE

This book will teach you to use the Powerful Task Rubric for Designing Student Work to analyze, design, and refine engaging tasks of learning.

JAYME LINTON

Designed to help K–5 teachers develop and implement a personalized plan for instruction in blended environments, this resource identifies key competencies and strategies for development.

LISA WESTMAN

Full of step-by-step guidance, this book shows you how to build collaborative student–teacher relationships and incorporate student voice and choice in the process of planning for student-driven differentiation.

CATLIN R. TUCKER, TIFFANY WYCOFF, AND JASON T. GREEN

Blended Learning in Action is the resource educators need to help them shift to a blended learning model and transform education for the 21st century.

CATLIN R. TUCKER

This road map to Common Core success includes specific recommendations for free apps and tech tools, step-by-step guidelines for meeting standards, and teacher-tested lesson ideas.

CATLIN R. TUCKER

This guide helps teachers integrate online with face-to-face instruction to personalize learning, increase engagement, and prepare students for high-stakes exams without sacrificing class time.

To order your copies, visit corwin.com

A SAGE Publishing Company

Helping educators make the greatest impact

CORWIN HAS ONE MISSION: to enhance education through intentional professional learning.

We build long-term relationships with our authors, educators, clients, and associations who partner with us to develop and continuously improve the best evidence-based practices that establish and support lifelong learning.

CPSIA information can be obtained
at www.ICGtesting.com
Printed in the USA
LVHW101512180521
687784LV00005B/227